P9-AOE-446

Brookings Occasional Papers

The New GATT
Implications for the United States

SUSAN M. COLLINS AND BARRY P. BOSWORTH, EDITORS

Andrew Carnegie Library
Livingstone College
701 W. Monroe St.
Salisbury, NC 28144

THE BROOKINGS INSTITUTION

Washington, D.C.

126484

Brookings Occasional Papers

THE BROOKINGS INSTITUTION is a private nonprofit organization devoted to research, education, and publication on important issues of domestic and foreign policy. Its principal purpose is to bring knowledge to bear on the major policy problems facing the American people.

On occasion Brookings produces research papers that warrant immediate circulation as contributions to the public debate on current issues of national importance. Because of the speed of their production, these Occasional Papers are not subjected to all of the formal review and verification procedures established for the Institution's research publications. As in all Brookings publications, the judgments, conclusions, and recommendations presented in the Papers are solely those of the authors and should not be attributed to the trustees, officers, or other staff members of the Institution.

Copyright ©1994 by
THE BROOKINGS INSTITUTION
1775 Massachusetts Avenue, N.W., Washington, D.C. 20036
All rights reserved

ISBN 0-8157-1029-1

Library of Congress Catalog Number 94-078692

9 8 7 6 5 4 3 2 1

Contents

Acknowledgments

On July 6, 1994, the Brookings Institution held a conference to examine the key issues involved in the GATT Uruguay Round of multilateral trade negotiations, concluded on December 15, 1993, and signed by President Clinton on April 15, 1994. One objective of the conference was to foster a more active discussion, particularly in light of the congressional vote on ratification that was about to take place. Each of the four papers presented examined the main issues involved in central portions of the Agreement: the economic effects of trade liberalization, agriculture, the World Trade Organization, and the new areas of services and intellectual property rights. Each paper was discussed by one or more individuals with alternative perspectives. This volume contains revised versions of the papers, the remarks of the commentators, and a summary of the general discussions from each session. A brief overview of the main issues is provided in the introductory chapter, written by the editors, Barry P. Bosworth and Susan M. Collins. Both are senior fellows in the Brookings Economic Studies program; Susan M. Collins is also associate professor of economics at Georgetown University.

The editors would like to thank members of the Brookings staff who contributed to this publication. In particular, Paige Oeffinger organized the conference, assisted by Kathleen McDill and Marc Steinberg. Paige Oeffinger also contributed to typing and organizing the final manuscript.

The views expressed in this book are those of the individual authors and conference participants and should not be ascribed to the trustees, officers, or other staff members of the Brookings Institution.

Introduction

Susan M. Collins and Barry P. Bosworth

Intense controversy surrounded the approval of the North American Free Trade Agreement (NAFTA). The lack of public discussion or academic review of the latest agreement negotiated under the General Agreement on Tariffs and Trade (GATT) is thus surprising. By almost any measure the new agreement will have a more pronounced effect on the U.S. economy than NAFTA. This is true even though the round has frequently been characterized as disappointing relative to the goals it established at its first meeting in Punta del Este, Uruguay, in 1986. The negative assessment arises principally from the absence of large immediate actions to liberalize trade through the reduction of tariffs and nontariff barriers. The traditional focus on barriers to merchandise trade is only a small element of the current agreement, however. In terms of the breadth of issues addressed, the Uruguay Round, the eighth negotiating round under the GATT system, was the most ambitious. Its accomplishments are considerable in broadening the range of trade issues subject to such negotiations and in the extensive efforts to provide more of an institutional framework for monitoring compliance with the agreement and resolving disputes.

A conference was held at the Brookings Institution on July 6, 1994, to review the major features of the agreement and to provide some assessment of its implications for the United States. The four papers presented at that conference, together with discussant comments, are reproduced in this volume. The major issues were covered in four sessions: (1) the likely economic effect of tariffs and quantitative restrictions, the traditional forms of liberalizing merchandise trade; (2) agriculture, where disputes among the major industrial economies over conflicting trade practices held up the negotiations for several years; (3) the new World Trade Organization (WTO), which is designed to provide both a unifying institutional

1

umbrella for the different agreements and the procedural structure for settlement of disputes; and (4) the new agreements governing trade in services, intellectual property rights, and foreign investment.

Economic Effects

Alan Deardorff reviews some estimates of the economic effects of the quantifiable portions of the Uruguay Round. He notes that this is actually a relatively small feature of the agreement and that tariffs, the traditional form of trade restriction, have already been reduced to low levels. The agreement emphasizes establishing a new institutional system for trade relations and extending the negotiations to new areas, such as services and intellectual property rights, where methods of evaluating the effects are still very primitive.

Industrial country tariffs are to be cut from an average of 6.4 percent to 4 percent over a five-year period. While the reductions for developing countries are smaller, a much larger percentage of their tariffs will be bound, meaning that they cannot be increased without consultation with other member countries. Tariffs will be completely eliminated for some major categories of trade. The greater change is in the area of nontariff barriers, which are to be converted to tariffs and then reduced in future years. For example, the Multi-Fiber Agreement (MFA), which constitutes a major restriction on the exports of developing countries, is to be completely phased out over a ten-year period. Voluntary export agreements (VERs), which the large economies used as a substitute for prohibited increases in tariffs to restrict imports from specific countries, are to be banned.

Efforts to quantify the effects of the changes are still in the preliminary stage because researchers do not have full information on the precise reductions in individual tariffs. Analysis based on computable general equilibrium (CGE) models suggests that the gains in improved resource allocation will ultimately raise the level of global output and incomes by about one percent (approximately $200 billion a year). In examining the transitional costs, as measured by the number of workers who would have to change employment, Deardorff estimates that about 0.2 percent of the U.S. work force (180,000) will change jobs as a result of the changes in patterns of trade. This compares with annual job changes for other reasons of 10 percent or more of the work force. Much of the discussion at the conference focused on these estimates. Some participants thought they represented a minimal measure of the benefits; they pointed out that models that allowed for less than perfect competition and for the dynamic effects of trade liberalization would produce larger estimates of the gains.

One issue that has arisen with regard to congressional ratification of the agreement is that the reduction in tariffs on imports will worsen the budget deficit by $2 billion to $3 billion a year. Since the agreement reduces taxes paid by Americans, it will, under the budget rules, require an offsetting increase in some other tax or a cut in expenditures. Some participants thought that the budget rules should be waived in this case because the tariff reduction will ultimately increase incomes and government tax revenues; others pointed out that such an approach would lead to budgetary chaos as every interest group argued that its proposed tax cut or expenditure program would be self-financing in the long run.

Agriculture

Tim Josling focuses on the agricultural agreement, a subject of sharp dispute that delayed completion of the Uruguay Round. In this area, the negotiators were unable to reach consensus on the type of sweeping reduction in trade barriers that some countries originally sought. Instead, they agreed on major changes in the operational rules and methods of measuring trade protection, hoping that they will provide a better basis for negotiating significant liberalization in future years. Josling examines three separate aspects of the agreement: import access, export competition, and domestic support programs.

The most significant change in market access is a provision to convert nontariff measures into tariffs, which are more transparent in their effects on trade, and to bind the levels of those tariffs. The introduction of the tariffs is likely to result in more protection at first. After conversion, countries are committed to reduce the tariffs by an average of 36 percent over six years, but there is considerable scope for countries to concentrate their tariff reduction in categories with little effect on actual trade flows. There are also exceptions that allow departures from the tariff schedules if imports exceed a maximum percentage of the average of the previous few years. While tariffs will provide a more explicit and transparent basis for future negotiations, the anticipated near-term growth in agricultural trade is expected to be quite small.

The agreement prohibits the introduction of new export subsidy measures, but maintains many of those now in existence. The value of existing subsidies is to be gradually reduced in future years. The major gain was in defining what constitutes a subsidy.

Some progress was also made in categorizing the extent to which domestic agricultural support programs distort trade. Total support payments are to be cut in future years, but the ceiling limitations are unlikely to be binding on either the United States or the European Community in the near future. Again, much of the effect is diluted by exceptions for specific practices of some of the largest industrial countries. The agreement also introduces new rules governing health standards on food products, an area that has generated considerable conflict in recent years, but there was some disagreement at the conference over the effectiveness of these regulations.

The major gains are in negotiating more effective rules and definitions, as well as explicit commitments by governments similar to those governing tariffs on nonagricultural trade. Optimists see this as a basis for more meaningful, formula-based reductions of trade barriers in the future. There is likely to be little immediate liberalization of trade, however.

The World Trade Organization and Dispute Resolution

The charter of the World Trade Organization represents a major change in the organizational structure of the GATT. The original GATT was negotiated in 1947-48 under the assumption that its organizational services would be provided by a proposed International Trade Organization (ITO). The ITO was not approved by the U.S. Congress because of concerns about its effect on U.S. sovereignty. In subsequent years the GATT encountered increasing problems because of ambiguity in its interpretation, and the system for resolving disputes never worked well. Furthermore, the old GATT comprised a large number of agreements. Some countries acceding to the GATT were able to select those agreements to which they wished to adhere. They could thus obtain the major benefit of most favored nation (MFN) status without complying with other portions of the GATT.

Under the new GATT, countries will have to agree, when they join the WTO, to abide by all of the individual agreements for which it is the unifying organization. The WTO is designed to formalize the rules and procedures of the old GATT and extend them to the new agreements on services and intellectual property rights. It also provides the institutional base for the new procedures aimed at dispute resolution. Nevertheless, the new WTO has very little real power because its rulings will not be legally binding on countries in the same sense as a treaty.

The WTO has aroused some concern about its effect on national sovereignty. John Jackson argues that this issue has been addressed by requirements for unanimity or super majorities. Furthermore, the organization has no powers to force compliance with its findings. As a last resort, countries can respond to decisions to which they are opposed by withdrawing from the GATT. Given the U.S. importance in the global trading system, it is hard to conceive that it could be forced to accept a ruling or amendments to which it is opposed.

The major change in the procedure for settling disputes is a clause that prevents countries from blocking the establishment of review panels. Nor will they be able to block adoption of a panel report to which they are opposed unless they can obtain a consensus in favor of their position. Thus countries will no longer be able simply to suppress complaints against their trade practices. Panel findings will not have legal standing in the United States, however, and the government will still have discretion in implementing the results.

Several participants expressed disappointment at the inability to make significant progress against the abuse of antidumping laws. It was also noted that the United States has used the implementing legislation of the Uruguay Round as a vehicle for changes in its trade laws that increase the restrictive effect of the antidumping provisions. Many of these changes were thought to be inconsistent with the spirit, and perhaps the rules, of the new international agreement.

Services and Intellectual Property Rights

Bernard Hoekman provides a comprehensive review of two new agreements, the General Agreement on Trade in Services (GATS) and the Agreement on Trade-Related Intellectual Property Rights (TRIPS). From a U.S. perspective, these may be the most important features of the Uruguay Round because they are so closely related to areas of American comparative advantage. Trade in nonfactor services now accounts for about one-fifth of global trade, and it is growing at nearly 10 percent annually. These agreements represent a major extension of GATT principles beyond the traditional area of trade in goods.

The GATS is only a first step, however, and it lacks some of the breadth that the United States had hoped would be applied to provisions mandating national treatment and nondiscrimination in services trade. Both in the United States and in other countries, interest groups emerged to oppose opening their sectors to full foreign competition. The GATS is similar to the GATT in its goal of formalizing rules and liberalizing access to markets. As with agriculture, it made more progress in establishing some basic principles and a framework for further negotiations than in achieving immediate reduction of trade barriers. MFN status was adopted as a general principle, but it is not yet applied unconditionally to all areas of services, as with trade in goods. Significant progress was also made in adopting a rule of *national treatment* in which foreign firms would be treated no worse than domestic service providers. It was more difficult, however, to agree on what constitutes barriers to access in services than in goods. The agreement also adopted a sectoral approach in which commitments are only applicable to specific listed service sectors.

The TRIPS is a different type of measure in that it actually restricts some forms of commerce to protect intellectual property rights. The major focus is on increased uniformity of countries' laws regarding copyright, trademark, and patent protection, which it accomplishes by seeking agreement to a set of minimum standards. Copyrights are to last for at least fifty years, and piracy is to be regarded as a criminal act. Patent protection is extended for twenty years. Countries must also ensure that they have credible enforcement programs.

Much of the discussion of the paper centered on whether strong patent protection was desirable. There were conflicting views on the effectiveness of patents in promoting innovation. Many developing countries perceive such actions as an attempt to restrict their access to modern technology and believe that the magnitude of monopoly rents granted to the holders of patents is excessive when extended to a global market.

A recurrent theme of the conference was what the participants saw as relatively small gains in immediate reductions in trade barriers, but some potentially significant improvements in the rules governing trade—particularly in services. Overall, the agreement was seen as dominated by the concerns of the large industrial economies. Developing countries were seen as joining, even though they may experience some short-term losses, because of their greater dependency on the global trade system. Finally, participants considered the likely future of multilateral trade negotiations. There is considerable scope for building on the groundwork established by the Uruguay Round Agreement, particularly in services and in further institutional development to facilitate international economic cooperation.

Economic Effects of Quota and Tariff Reductions

Alan V. Deardorff

The Uruguay Round is a remarkable and important achievement, not because it will change the world, but because it will permit the world to continue to change for the better for other reasons. The round itself, at least in its economic effects, may not make a big difference. Its effects on the world economy will be largely beneficial, but those effects that economists have been able to quantify are rather small, while the sizes of other effects are necessarily uncertain. If these effects, estimates of which I will survey in this paper, were the only reason for the Uruguay Round, then skeptics might be excused for doubting that it was worth the seven years of effort that produced it. Those who expect negative side effects on their particular pet portions of the world economy might be justified in resenting such costs in return for so little gain.

The importance of the Uruguay Round, however, lies instead in the many beneficial changes in the world economy that it will permit to continue. By preserving the momentum of trade liberalization that began almost fifty years ago under the GATT and by extending the liberal market principles of the GATT to many new sectors of the economy never touched before, the Uruguay Round permits the vast majority of the world's governments to reaffirm the importance of these principles and forces them to restrain somewhat their natural inclination to muck things up. The Uruguay Round, like the GATT, which preceded it, is hardly perfect. But the overwhelming message of the round is that self-destructive

My thanks to Drusilla Brown, Bernard Hoekman, John Jackson, and Bob Stern for their helpful comments and conversations on the topic of this paper and to my discussants, Thea Lea and Bob Lawrence, and to other participants at the Brookings meeting. Partial financial support was provided by the Ford Foundation.

government intervention in the international economy is to be curtailed. This message, conveyed internationally through the improved mechanism for set- tling disputes, will reassure markets and permit the great progress that has already been made in market economies to continue and to spread.

Progress is evident on so many fronts that it is perhaps taken for granted. The great market economies of the world have grown so rapidly in the past fifty years that any slowing of that unprecedented growth, or dislocations that accompany it, are sometimes taken as signs that the system is not working. Yet it is only the success of the system during the early postwar years that makes the current less rapid pace of economic growth appear a failure. Problems must be addressed, of course. But to turn back en masse from liberal trade and the market mechanism would only make those problems worse. The Uruguay Round is the world's way of committing to those market principles and ensur- ing that solutions to problems will be sought in ways that will enhance world welfare rather than doing so at the expense of others.

In the past fifteen years, one after another of the world's developing econo- mies has recognized and then demonstrated the benefits of using the market, rather than resisting it, in promoting development. They have been followed by other developing economies that are only now getting that message and by current and former communist countries that have also begun the same process. All of these countries depend on world markets' remaining open, or their already difficult efforts to turn their economies around will become impossible. Again, the Uruguay Round is in no way responsible for these changes, but if it had failed, they too would have become that much more difficult to attain.

I mention all of this because my topic is the likely economic effects of the Uruguay Round, and these are routinely estimated to be rather small. The danger in pointing this out is that those opposed to the round will argue that the benefits of the round are therefore small and outweighed by other considera- tions, and that even those in favor of the round will find their motivation dampened. But this, in my view, would miss the point entirely. The success of the round is critical in continuing to foster the atmosphere of liberal trade and market incentives that is responsible for half a century of economic progress. It is not so much that the round will hasten this progress as that failure of the round could cause it to reverse direction.

This does not mean that the economic effects of the Uruguay Round are less worthy of examination. Many tout its benefits, but many others fear the effects of trade liberalization, expecting it to cause serious dislocations in the markets, such as labor markets, that they care most about. As we will see, however, for the same reasons that analyses suggest that the overall economic benefits of the round will be small, they also suggest that these dislocations will be small and manageable. Therefore, if I am right that the greater importance of the round is not its economic effects per se, but rather its role in permitting continued progress in the world economy more generally, then the only ones who should fear the round are not those who think they stand to lose from trade, but those who stand to lose from broader economic progress.

Overview of the Uruguay Round

The Uruguay Round Agreement is a massive document including many more provisions than I can mention here. The most important are shown in box 1–1.

Tariffs

At the top of the list are tariff cuts. These, which have been the staple of the GATT since its beginning, are still an important component even though previous rounds have already brought tariffs down to historically low levels. Average industrial country tariffs are only 6.4 percent, and, while these will be reduced by 39 percent, this only brings them down to an average of 4.0 percent. This average reduction of only two and a half percentage points could hardly be expected to cause large changes in the aggregate, though since particular tariffs will be reduced much more, the effects in particular sectors will be more significant. The cuts include complete elimination of tariffs in a number of sectors, including steel, pharmaceuticals, construction equipment, agricultural equipment, and medical equipment, and they include substantial reductions in other sectors, such as semiconductors and computers. Many of these sectors are of obvious importance to the United States, and indeed there is considerable enthusiasm for the round in the U.S. export industries, where the largest of these tariff cuts are expected to make a difference.

Developing countries have undertaken to reduce tariffs by less than have the industrialized countries, with the result that the average tariff reduction for all countries in the round is closer to the one-third reduction that was the target of the negotiations.[1] Even for developing countries, however, the round is still a major

---

1. I have seen several different numbers reported, presumably based on different decisions about whom and what to include and what weights to use. Access to the numbers themselves has so far been delayed, at least for those of us outside government, by reluctance of some participating countries to release them.

Box 1-1. Main Features of the Uruguay Round

Tariff cuts

Tariffs on industrial goods will be cut by a trade-weighted average of 34 percent (39 percent by industrial countries), reducing average industrial country tariffs from 6.4 percent to 4.0 percent. Cuts include complete elimination of tariffs in several sectors (for example, construction, agricultural, and medical equipment; steel; pharmaceuticals) and deep cuts in other sectors (for example, semiconductors and computers). Most reductions will be phased in over five years.

Agriculture

Export subsidies will be reduced by 36 percent in value; domestic supports (except some "green box" subsidies) will be reduced by 20 percent; nontariff barriers will be converted to tariffs ("tariffication"); and average industrial-country tariffs will be cut by 36 percent over six years.

Textiles and clothing

The Multifiber Arrangement will be phased out. Importing countries are to integrate groups of products into the GATT in four stages over ten years. Meanwhile, existing quota restrictions are to be expanded at minimum growth rates.

Rules

Rules for Safeguards, Antidumping, and Subsidies have been revised. *Safeguards:* Voluntary Export Restraints are to be eliminated; compensation is no long required; selective safeguards are permitted but only in exceptional circumstances. *Antidumping:* Rules for calculating dumping margins are improved; "sunset" provision restricts duties to five years; there are new provisions for anti-circumvention. *Subsidies:* Classified as Prohibited ("red box"), for example, export subsidies; Actionable ("yellow box"), for example, if they cause injury; and Non-Actionable ("green box"), for example, assistance for research and regional subsidies.

---

accomplishment, for it has expanded the percentage of imports covered by tariff bindings—the ceilings above which they commit not to raise future rates—from a negligible 12 percent to more than 50 percent. This is symptomatic of another important change in this round compared with previous rounds: the developing countries are no longer being accorded the dubious favor of exemption from many of its provisions. The reason for this, of course, is the recent recognition by many developing countries of the benefits of trade liberalization.

Nontariff Barriers

Nontariff barriers (NTBs) were addressed in a small way in the previous round, the Tokyo Round, of multilateral trade negotiations, but the Uruguay Round is the first to tackle the major NTBs head on and to make a determined

---

Trade-Related Intellectual Property Rights (TRIPS)

The agreement provides minimum standards for protection of intellectual property, including trademarks, patents, and copyrights.

Trade-Related Investment Measures (TRIMS)

A number of TRIMS are identified as inconsistent with GATT and must be eliminated within two years by industrial countries, five years by developing countries, and seven years by least developed countries. Prohibited TRIMS include local content requirements and trade balancing requirements.

Services

A new agreement, the General Agreement on Trade in Services (GATS), requires national treatment and most favored nation treatment, with some specified exceptions, for trade and investment in those services sectors covered by the agreement; it also provides a framework for further negotiations on services. Sectors on which progress was made include professional services and telecommunications services; financial services are subject to continuing negotiations during the first six months of the agreement.

Dispute settlement mechanism

The GATT dispute settlement mechanism is unified and strengthened, eliminating the current practice of permitting one country (often the defendant) to block a panel report. New procedures include a right of retaliation against a member that does not comply with panel recommendations, plus a binding appellate review process.

World Trade Organization (WTO)

This new institution combines almost all features of the old and new GATTs, as well as the Tokyo Round Codes, into a single organization, membership in which implies acceptance of all elements. Membership in the WTO will raise and extend the obligations of developing countries. The WTO will provide for regular ministerial meetings, surveillance of members' trade policies, centralized notification of trade measures, and collaboration and cooperation with the World Bank and International Monetary Fund.

*Principal source: World Bank, "The Uruguay Round: A Preliminary Assessment," February 1994.

---

effort to remove them. The major NTBs are the quotas in textiles and apparel; quotas, subsidies, and other policies in agriculture; and the voluntary export restraints that exist in a variety of sectors such as steel and autos. The general approach of the Uruguay Round is to subject these NTBs to tariffication, converting them to tariffs that are then to be reduced, or to require that their effectiveness in their current form be modified by scheduled reductions in the extent to which they distort the markets. I have real doubts that this process will work as effectively as intended. But to have made these commitments at all in these sectors, which until now have been exempted from GATT discipline, is a remarkable achievement. Even if the actual progress in removing these barriers turns out to be disappointing, the commitment itself should be enough to reverse the continued proliferation that until now has paralleled the successful efforts to liberalize trade in other sectors.

In textiles and apparel, the NTBs have consisted of the complex of import quotas incorporated in the Multifiber Arrangement (MFA). This arrangement, which restricts the imports from only developing countries, has displayed inexorable growth in both the countries and the commodities covered since its predecessor arrangement took effect in 1963. At the same time that it has attempted to protect producers in the industrialized countries, the arrangement has provided guaranteed market shares to many established LDC producers. The greatest costs have therefore been borne by developed country consumers of low-end textile and apparel products, and by the least developed countries when they have tried to enter these markets. The Uruguay Round undertakes to phase this arrangement out completely over the next ten years, both by a scheduled expansion of the quotas themselves (to make them less restrictive) and by requiring importing countries to shift groups of products in four stages out of the arrangement and into conventional GATT treatment. Unfortunately, this process is very much "back loaded," with 49 percent of products due to be moved into the GATT only in the tenth year and with importing countries permitted to make their own selections of which products to move in the earlier stages.

Agriculture has been subject to a much wider variety of NTBs, including policies that are not really barriers at all, but subsidies of production and trade. Together with more conventional quotas, outright prohibitions on imports of particular products, price support schemes, and the European variable levy, the trade policy landscape in agriculture has been a nightmare of inefficiencies ever since it was exempted from GATT discipline (at U.S. insistence) shortly after the GATT began. Agricultural subsidies were one of the major sticking points of the Uruguay Round negotiations, the United States and other agricultural exporters insisting on much greater reductions in these subsidies than the Europeans, especially the French, were willing to consider. In the end the Uruguay Round achieved commitments for only partial reductions in these and other agricultural NTBs, but these reductions are not that much smaller than, say, the tariff reductions mentioned above. And, like so much else in the Uruguay Round, the greatest achievement may be to have them included in the agreement at all.

Voluntary export restraints (VERs) have been used in a number of sensitive sectors, especially by the United States and Europe, primarily as an alternative to providing safeguards protection under article XIX of the GATT. Because article XIX required compensation and did not permit protection to be levied selectively against countries that were the source of an increase in imports, importing countries turned instead to VERs, which are negotiated bilaterally with the exporting countries. The Uruguay Round eliminates these VERs and prohibits their use in the future. Rules for safeguards are being relaxed, no longer requiring compensation and permitting some selectivity, in return for multilateral surveillance and a sunset provision. The hope is that countries will now follow these rules rather than circumventing them through VERs.

Rules

Others of the GATT rules have also been renegotiated, specifically those concerning antidumping and subsidies/countervailing duties. These rules regarding so-called unfair trade and the actions taken under them have grown in importance over the past decade, so that antidumping duties and countervailing duties are arguably the remedy of choice for most industries seeking assistance in a growing list of countries. The Uruguay Round has addressed these rules, though with mixed results.

Pressures for reform of antidumping laws were as much directed at increasing their restraint of trade as at reducing it. The agreement therefore includes both new anticircumvention rules, which will extend antidumping duties to types of trade not previously covered, and tightened rules on defining dumping and measuring dumping margins, which will eliminate some of the more egregious uses of antidumping laws. Whether the net effect of these changes will be to expand or to contract the use of antidumping is hard to say.

The main change in subsidies is the adoption of the "traffic light" approach. This explicitly identifies three categories of subsidies based on their severity and the actions that may be taken against them. The "red box" defines subsidies that are simply prohibited, such as export subsidies. The "yellow box" defines subsidies that are permitted but are actionable; for example, if they cause injury, they may be subject to countervailing duties. The "green box," finally, defines subsidies that are nonactionable. These include nonspecific subsidies, assistance for certain research activities, regional subsidies, and assistance to meet environmental requirements.

New Issues

Right from the beginning a distinguishing and ambitious feature of the Uruguay Round was the intent to deal with a series of completely new issues that had never before been subject to negotiation under the GATT. Two of these—Trade-Related Intellectual Property Rights (TRIPs) and Trade-Related Investment Measures (TRIMs)—were to be incorporated into the GATT even though neither involved such direct interference with trade flows as had the previous issues addressed in the GATT. The services issue, in contrast, was felt initially to require a separate agreement—the General Agreement on Trade in Services (GATS)—although the outcome of the round was to include both GATS and GATT under the umbrella of a single World Trade Organization and linked by a single mechanism for settling disputes.

The TRIPs agreement extends and harmonizes the rules and procedures for providing patents, copyrights, trademarks, and other forms of intellectual property protection. This was a high priority item for the United States in entering the negotiations, motivated by the owners of such forms of intellectual property who were being undermined by absent or lax protection abroad. Early in the negotiations many developing countries resisted agreement on TRIPs, seeing it primarily as a way to extract monopoly profits from their consumers. Many of these countries, however, later came to believe that they too might benefit from the stimulus to innovation and creative activity that intellectual property protection can provide.

The TRIMs agreement deals with policies used to restrict or to control foreign direct investment that in turn affect trade. Most important among these are local content requirements, which require investors to use a certain fraction of locally supplied inputs (which might otherwise be imported), and trade balancing requirements that call on investors to export as much as they import. Both of these policies will be prohibited, explicitly reaffirming articles III and XI of the GATT as applied to investment issues.

The services agreement opens up a whole new category of international transactions to international discipline. While many would argue that the economic principles that underlie trade in services are the same as those that underlie trade in goods, the fact that services do not cross national borders in easily identified physical form has meant that they have been subject to policies that are quite different from the tariffs and quotas that have been the traditional focus of the GATT. At the same time, international trade in many services requires at least some presence by the service provider in the importing country, and this means that trade in services raises issues of international investment and migration that, at least until the TRIMs agreement, have been absent from the GATT. The new GATS attempts to extend many of the principles of the GATT to services sectors, however, including the nondiscrimination principles of most favored nation and national treatment. The coverage of the agreement is less than had been hoped, but it still represents a breakthrough in establishing the principle that services transactions should not be exempt from international rules and in providing a mechanism for further negotiations to liberalize them in the future.

Institutional Framework

The final, and in many ways the most important, accomplishment of the Uruguay Round was to provide an improved institutional framework for overseeing and enforcing the other parts of the agreement and for extending and refining it in the future. The new dispute settlement mechanism and the World Trade Organization (WTO) both should enhance the confidence of the participating countries that these agreements will alter behavior.

The mechanism for settling disputes continues to use the same sorts of panels to decide cases as have been used for years under the GATT. Now, however, there will be a single such mechanism for all parts of the agreement instead of separate mechanisms for each, as was the case after the Tokyo Round. More important, it will no longer be possible for a single country, often the defendant in a dispute, to block the establishment of a panel or the adoption of a panel report. A panel decision will thus automatically go into effect unless it is appealed under a new binding appellate review process. Of course no mechanism in international law can force a sovereign nation into complying with such a decision, but the fact that a country cannot now block an adverse decision and then ignore it on the pretense that it never occurred, and that other countries will now be more readily permitted to retaliate if the panel decision is ignored, will put teeth into the new rules that were never present before.

Finally, the creation of the new WTO will put all of these international agreements and mechanisms into an institutional framework that has been lacking during the forty-year history of the GATT. Because the GATT was intended only as an interim agreement, awaiting the proposed International Trade Organization that was never approved, the GATT has never had an institutional structure adequate to its purpose.[2] The WTO will correct that, combining those aspects of the old GATT that have not been amended with everything that has been negotiated in the Uruguay Round, including the GATS, into a single organization. Membership in that organization will imply

---

2. See Jackson (1989) for the history on this.

acceptance of all of these elements, for all countries including developing countries, and there will be no more "free riding."[3] The new WTO will provide for regular ministerial meetings, surveillance of members' trade policies, centralized notification of trade measures, and collaboration and cooperation with the World Bank and the International Monetary Fund.

Timing

All of the foregoing will take time to implement, of course. The tariff reductions on industrial products will be phased in by means of five equal reductions over a period of five years. Liberalization in agriculture will take six years for industrial countries and ten years for developing countries. As already noted, the elimination of the Multifiber Arrangement will take ten years, with almost half of the quotas eliminated only in the tenth year, though the explicit schedule for growth of quotas for each of the preceding ten years may make many of these quotas irrelevant before that.

Existing safeguards are to be eliminated in five to eight years and existing VERs in four years, though each member country can retain one VER until the end of 1999. Prohibited subsidies are to be phased out over periods of five to eight years. There is also a "sunset" provision that eliminates antidumping duties after five years unless they are justified by a review.

Under the TRIPs agreement, national treatment and most favored nation treatment will be implemented for developing countries one year after the WTO is established, though implementation of new intellectual property protection may be delayed by four or more years for developing countries, and by ten or more years by least developed countries. Investment measures are to be eliminated within two years, with longer periods for developing countries. And while the nondiscrimination principle under the GATS goes into effect immediately, countries can register numerous exemptions from it that are to be reviewed after five years and eliminated, in principle, after ten.

As these observations indicate, then, the implementation of the Uruguay Round will be a gradual process, and one should not expect the immediate removal of many barriers to trade. On the other hand, gradual but predictable implementation should make it relatively easy for countries to deal with any

---

3. Though exceptions are written into some of the agreements for the least developed countries.

disruptions that liberalization will entail, and the benefits of GATT discipline on any new actions by governments will, of course, be in place immediately.

Measurements of the Economic Effects of the Uruguay Round

Efforts to quantify the economic effects of the Uruguay Round began early in the negotiations, when it was expected that agreement would be reached much earlier than it was. Thus several studies were completed as early as 1990, and they attempted to anticipate the quantifiable results of the round. The delay in the negotiations then put such analyses on hold, and a second spate of studies appeared near the end of the negotiations in 1993. None of these studies, however, has yet been able to take into account the final results of the round, for the exact reductions in tariffs and other barriers to trade that were negotiated have not yet been made public. All studies have therefore had to work either with guesses as to what the results might be, or with preliminary versions of the agreement that became available late in the negotiation process.

This inaccuracy in the data on the outcome of the negotiations is small, however, compared with another uncertainty of these calculations: most of what was negotiated is not susceptible to quantitative analysis. Of the nine features of the Uruguay Round that are listed in box 1–1, only the first three—tariff reductions and relaxations of NTBs in agriculture and textiles/apparel—can even conceptually be quantified with existing economic models. And even here, the measurement of NTBs is notoriously difficult, so that studies have had to rely primarily on inventories of where NTBs are present. None of the other features of the round, important as most analysts believe them to be, have been measured or modeled in anything like a general way.

The studies that have been done are nonetheless useful for indicating some bounds on potential effects of the Uruguay Round. To give some sense of what (primarily other) investigators have found about these bounds, I report in table 1–1 a selection of results from the literature for effects of the Uruguay Round on welfare, trade, employment, and economic dislocation.

The sources of these estimates are a group of papers listed at the bottom of the table. They include all of the papers that I have seen that attempt to evaluate the tariff and NTB liberalization of the Uruguay Round for all goods sectors.[4] All of

---

4. None of the papers attempt to quantify liberalization in services. Many other papers have focused on only a few sectors, especially agriculture, but I have not included them here.

them are based on so-called computable general equilibrium (CGE) models of the economy, the differences among them being primarily in the ways that they have divided up the industries and countries of the world and, more important, their guesses about policy changes the Uruguay Round may entail. In selecting and interpreting the numbers I have made some effort to scale down results that were based on assumptions of 100 percent tariff removal, for example. But otherwise I have reported the estimates much as they are. Even where the different studies disagree substantially, my sense is that the implications of their estimates are much the same, though readers may come to their own judgments.

All of these studies are based on assumptions of perfect competition and constant returns to scale in all markets. These are not obviously valid assumptions, by any means, and I offer some thoughts on how results might change if they were altered. With perfect competition, the models also typically use some variant of the "Armington Assumption"—that goods are differentiated by country of origin—in order to replicate the two-way trade flows and relative unresponsiveness of trade to price changes that are observed in the data.

Finally, these models are static. The are based completely on stationary supply and demand functions, and the models simply calculate the changes, from one static market equilibrium to the next, resulting from changing trade policies. This is important for understanding the models' results. When a model says that global GDP will rise by, say, one percent, it does not mean that the world's growth *rate* will rise by one percentage point, with GDP then rising one percent faster each year over the previous year. It means instead that, after all of the policy changes have worked themselves out, the world will achieve a new *level* of GDP that will be (and remain) one percent higher than it otherwise would have been.

Thus the models do not allow for what are often called "dynamic effects," such as the effects of possible increased capital accumulation or technical progress, except to the extent that these are implicit in movements along static supply and demand functions. Many would view this as a serious limitation of these analyses, and I offer some thoughts on this subject as well. For the time being, let us look at the results as they have been reported, since they are the best that we have available.

In table 1–1, I distinguish between permanent and transitional effects of the Uruguay Round. Most of the effects are permanent, reflecting changes in welfare, trade, and employment that will take some time to occur but that will remain with us after the round is implemented, presumably indefinitely. Transitional effects, on the other hand, refer to the changes that must take

Table 1-1. Estimates of the Economic Effects of the Uruguay Round

Permant effects of the Uruguay Round	Changes by end of implementation period
Increase in real global GDP[a,c,d,e,f,g] (= $140 billion–260 billion per year[1])	0.7–1.3 percent
Increase in real GDP by selected country[f]	
Smallest (ROW—chiefly least developed countries)	0.6 percent
United States (= $36.4 billion[1])	0.8 percent
Japan	2.0 percent
Largest (Non-EC western Europe)	2.1 percent
Increase in global trade[a,b,c,f] (= $250 billion–1 trillion per year[1])	5–20 percent
Sectors where value of trade will expand most[c]	
Clothing, footwear, and luggage	60.2 percent
Textiles	34.4 percent
Agriculture, forestry, and fisheries	20.3 percent
Sectors/countries where employment will change most[f]	20.3 percent
Light industries (inc. textiles & apparel)	
United States[2]	–36 percent
Asian NICs (Hong Kong, Korea, Taiwan, Singapore)	+83 percent
Agriculture	
Japan	–21 percent
Australia and New Zealand	+3.6 percent

Transitional effects of the Uruguay Round	Spread over implementation period
Labor Market Dislocation for the World[b] (= 5 million–7 million workers)	0.7–1.0 percent
Labor market dislocation by country[b]	
United States (= 180,000 workers)	0.2 percent
Other developed countries	
Least (Canada)	0.5 percent
Most (Japan)	4.1 percent
Less developed countries	
Least (India)	0.2 percent
Most (Hong Kong)	12.3 percent

Sources:
a. Burniaux and others (1990).
b. Deardorff and Stern (1990).
c. Francois, McDonald, and Nordström (1993).
d. Goldin, Knudsen, and van der Mansbrugghe (1993).
e. Nguyen, Perroni, and Wigle (1991).
f. Nguyen, Perroni, and Wigle (1993).
g. OECD (1993).
Notes:
1. Dollar values are very approximate, valued at (possibly different and approximate) early 1990s prices and incomes.
2. But note that Deardorff and Stern (1990) get contraction of U.S. apparel employment of only 0.8 percent and a 0.04 percent *expansion* of the U.S. textile industry.

place to get from here to there, changes that will be spread out over the period of implementation but that will stop once the new equilibrium is attained. In principle, these transitional effects would include the costs to the economy of shifting capital from declining to expanding industries, of retraining workers to match the new skills required of a new output mix, even the administrative costs of dealing with these shifts through policies of adjustment assistance. In practice, the table reports only the dislocations that may be expected in labor markets. These will be explained further.

Permanent Effects

The most fundamental measure of the effect of the Uruguay Round is the measure of economic welfare, or real GDP. Of the studies included here, all but one have reported effects on global welfare, with the range of estimates reported in the first line of table 1–1. The percentage effects are centered on a one percent increase in global GDP, ranging from about one-third less to one-third more than this. These changes translate into dollar changes of between $140 billion and $260 billion a year.[5]

Are these changes large or small? In percentage terms remember that this is the new *level* of world GDP that will be achieved only after the implementation period of five to ten years—the gain looks quite small. Compared with all of the other changes that will undoubtedly be occurring over that same period and with the growth that one hopes will occur for other reasons, this gradual, once-and-for-all increase of one percent or so will hardly be noticed.

Nevertheless, even the lower estimate of $140 billion a year is not peanuts. Viewed as an exercise in cost-benefit analysis, a $140 billion-a-year dividend, even after five or ten years, more than justifies the seven years of effort that went into the round. A better question, however, is whether these gains are enough to justify the costs that will be borne by those who lose from the round.

The table also reports a few results for the effects of the round on real incomes of separate countries.[6] These derive from Nguyen and others, whose model divided the world into ten countries and regions. With this level of aggregation, all of the ten benefit from the round, the smallest benefit being felt in percentage terms by a large rest-of-world grouping that includes chiefly least developed countries, and the greatest benefit going to a grouping of western European countries outside of the European Union (EU). But the range of changes runs only from 0.6 percent to 2.1 percent, and therefore really does not represent great diversity in the welfare effects of the round by country.

The greatest attention often focuses on a trade agreement's effects on trade itself, even though I would argue that these are the least important. Trade is

---

5. Or in some cases the figures that were reported were in dollars, and I have done my best to infer the corresponding percentage.

6. Nguyen, Perroni, and Wigle (1993).

only a means to the end of raising consumer welfare, and attention should be placed on those changes in welfare and how they are distributed. Nonetheless, I do report in table 1–1 some of the estimates that have appeared for the effects of the Uruguay Round on trade. These are much larger, in percentage terms, than the effects on welfare, ranging for global trade from 5 to 20 percent expansion, depending on which of four studies is the source. Thus the trade liberalization that is contained in the Uruguay Round Agreement is indeed expected to provide a substantial stimulus to trade. This is not surprising, I suppose, but, recalling that the largest countries only reduce their tariffs from 6.4 percent to 4.0 percent, this could not have been taken for granted.

Because existing trade barriers are very uneven, one expects this increase in trade to be far from uniform. Indeed, as reported in table 1–1, trade expands a great deal more than average in certain sectors, most notably apparel (60.2 percent) and textiles (34.4 percent).[7] Francois and others also report a substantial increase in agricultural trade, though here the fact that the round combines trade liberalization with removal of certain subsidies to trade has a dampening effect.

Finally, to give a sense of how the fortunes of various national industries will change due to the round, I report the net employment changes that are estimated by Nguyen and his colleagues for those sector and country pairs that contract or expand the most.[8] As the growth of trade would suggest, the largest changes are in "light industries," which, in the classification developed by Nguyen and others, includes primarily textiles and apparel. Here employment is estimated to contract by 36 percent in the United States and to expand by 83 percent in the Asian newly industrialized countries (NICs). I suspect that these are somewhat smaller changes than some would have expected, based on the popular perception of that sector's vulnerability to trade in the industrialized countries. Even these numbers are very large, however, compared with the figures proposed by Deardorff and Stern, who estimate a contraction of U.S. employment in the apparel industry of less than one percent and actually get a tiny *expansion* of the U.S. textile industry.[9]

Also reported in table 1–1 are employment changes in agriculture, which according to Nguyen and others will contract the most in Japan (-21 percent).[10]

---

7. Francois, McDonald, and Nordström (1993).
8. Nguyen, Perroni, and Wigle (1993).
9. The textile industry includes, of course, many synthetics that are quite capital intensive and thus do well in the United States.
10. Nguyen, Perroni, and Wigle (1993).

They find agricultural employment expanding the most in Australia and New Zealand, but by a comparatively small (for them) 3.6 percent.

Transitional Effects

As I have stressed, the gains in real income are permanent changes but will take time to appear. Meanwhile, in order to accomplish the changes in employment by industry that were just mentioned, some workers will have to adjust. These adjustment costs are not part of any of the models used to study the Uruguay Round, but one can easily get some idea of what is involved by looking at the sizes of the adjustments that must be achieved. If one believes, for example, the 36 percent reduction in textile and apparel employment reported above, 36 percent of the current workers in that industry will have to find employment elsewhere by the time the round is implemented. This may look like quite a lot, but one must remember that this is only one industry among many, so the workers involved may be only a small fraction of the total labor force. Furthermore, they will have five or ten years (ten at least, in the case of textiles) to make the adjustment.

To provide a broader measure of these labor-market adjustments, therefore, Deardorff and Stern calculated what we called the "gross change in employment" for the trade round.[11] Assuming, as most of these studies do, that aggregate employment is held fixed, we calculated for each country the sum of just the contractions in employment (which therefore equaled, by assumption, the sum of expansions). This is therefore a measure of how many workers will have to change industries of employment as a result of the round. It is a far from perfect measure of labor market dislocation, of course. It does not capture, for example, the extent to which these workers will have to be retrained in order to find work in their new industries, which could employ workers with the same mix of skills as the old, or very different. Nor does it does capture the extent to which workers will have to move to different locations, which will depend on how expanding and contracting industries are distributed geographically.[12] So we do not really know how burdensome this labor market dislocation is.

For the world as a whole (adding up the gross employment changes for all countries), we calculate that from 5 to 7 million workers will have to change

---

11. Deardorff and Stern (1990).
12. These are issues that we have dealt with for the NAFTA in Brown, Deardorff, and Stern (1992), but have not had occasion to do yet for the Uruguay round.

industries of employment as a result of the Uruguay Round, depending on the assumptions that we make about what the round will entail. That is a lot of people, especially if you are one of them, but it is no more than one percent of the world's labor force. Since these changes will be spread over the entire implementation period, one might expect only one- or two-tenths of one percent of workers to be dislocated in a given year. This is negligible compared with normal labor-market turnover.

I also report in table 1–1 these labor market dislocation estimates for selected other countries, noting those for the United States as well as the largest and smallest estimates among other developed and developing countries. The largest estimate of dislocation is for Hong Kong, where more than 12 percent of workers are expected to change industries.

I noted at the outset that the quantifiable effects of the Uruguay Round would be relatively small, and the numbers in table 1–1 show this. This is not surprising to those of us who have spent much time modeling the effects of trade liberalization in general equilibrium; it has been true routinely for other liberalizations, from the EC many years ago to the Tokyo Round and the NAFTA more recently. In part this occurs because the reductions in trade barriers themselves are never as large as one might have expected. The average tariff reductions in the Uruguay Round for the industrialized countries were only 2.4 percentage points and, while the reductions for the developing countries with larger initial tariffs were larger, this does not provide a very large change. Nontariff barriers are larger, in many cases, but they typically apply to only a small part of trade, and their liberalization is only partial or delayed.

Equally important, though, is the fact that, in a general equilibrium model, the separate changes in tariffs and NTBs have a strong tendency to cancel each other out. General equilibrium interactions among sectors and countries cause increases in costs and reductions in demand that offset what one might have expected from examination of only the most obvious partial equilibrium effects of a tariff or quota. Indeed, one of the main findings of CGE models when they were first being developed in the 1970s was that they generated substantially smaller estimates of the effects of trade liberalization than the partial equilibrium models that had preceded them, and for good reasons.

The static, perfectly competitive CGE models are also believed to have biases in the downward direction compared with what might be found with models that are dynamic or that incorporate imperfect competition and increasing returns to scale.

Biases in the Models

Several CGE models have now been developed that incorporate aspects of imperfect competition, increasing returns to scale, and the dynamics of investment. These have not, to my knowledge, been applied to the Uruguay Round. Given the nature of these issues, we are far from having a consensus on what models should look like, so perhaps this is just as well. But some comparison of these second-generation models with the static competitive ones can nonetheless indicate the extent of the biases that the latter may include.

Imperfect Competition and Increasing Returns to Scale

The first attempt to include these features of the new trade theory into a CGE model of trade was by Harris and Cox.[13] At issue was the U.S.-Canada Free Trade Agreement (FTA), and Harris and Cox built a model of Canada that ingeniously incorporated two models of imperfect competition. Their results for the welfare effects of the FTA for Canada were about ten times larger than the estimates coming out of perfectly competitive models, and this appears to have been a persuasive piece of evidence in favor of the FTA in the Canadian debate.

The Harris-Cox modeling approach has not been followed by other investigators, however, because it was criticized on conceptual grounds. It was not clear, for example, that the two models of imperfect competition that it combined were consistent with one another, and some suspected that this peculiar structure of the model contributed to the results. Others have therefore taken a different approach to including imperfect competition in CGE models.

Brown and Stern, for example, produced a model of the United States and Canada, also directed at the U.S.-Canada FTA, that assumed a monopolistically competitive structure for manufacturing sectors.[14] They, too, found larger welfare and other effects from the FTA using this model than they had gotten from a perfectly competitive model, but the bias was much smaller: effects were only two or three times as large. This same structure has since been applied by Brown and others to a model of the NAFTA; again, in orders of magnitude most of the results are not all that different from competitive models.[15]

---

13. Harris and Cox (1984).
14. Brown and Stern (1989).
15. Brown, Deardorff, and Stern (1992).

There is a long way to go, of course, before we will have a good idea of how imperfect competition and increasing returns to scale really matter for the effects of trade policy. We can, however, be fairly confident that the Harris-Cox estimate—that effects go up by a factor of ten—is an upper limit. Thus, for example, one can argue that, allowing for these factors, the global welfare effects of the round will be at most ten percent of GDP and most likely quite a bit smaller.

Dynamic Effects

Ever since economists calculated disappointingly small welfare effects to be expected from the formation of the European Community, they and others have stressed that there were undoubtedly other effects, usually termed "dynamic," that would make these effects larger even though we were unable to model them. This is surely plausible, and the experience of the EC countries in the early years, and of trade-liberalizing NICs more recently, are all strongly suggestive that freer trade stimulates economic progress in ways that are not captured in static models.

For a long time, however, trade theorists had little success in establishing a rigorous theoretical link between trade and growth, and this hampered any efforts to develop empirically based techniques to estimate the effect. The classic Solow neoclassical growth model, for example, produced a steady-state growth rate that was not even sensitive to the rate of saving, let alone to trade. Two recent developments in the theoretical literature, however, have moved us closer to the goal of linking trade and growth.

The first development was the revival of growth theory in the form of the so-called "endogenous growth" models initiated by Romer and Lucas.[16] These, by allowing for increasing returns to scale, were able to escape the straight-jacket of Solow's steady-state growth. Extended to an international context by Grossman and Helpman, these models have begun to provide plausible theoretical stories of how more open trade might permanently stimulate growth.[17] Unfortunately, these models are rather complex, and there is no consensus as to which of several mechanisms for endogenous growth are most likely to operate in the real world. For both of these reasons, the construction of CGE models

---

16. Romer (1986) and Lucas (1988).
17. Grossman and Helpman (1991).

that would contain these effects is only beginning, and it is too early to tell how large (and how likely) the effects will be.

The second development was a clever argument by Baldwin, who noted that even without an effect on the steady-state rate of growth, the income benefits of more open trade could translate into higher savings and higher investment that would lead, even in the Solow model, to an extra boost in income compared with the static model.[18] Baldwin argued that on this basis alone the welfare effects of trade liberalization should be scaled up by from 15 to 90 percent. This may not be a valid conclusion for some countries since, as Mazumdar has noted, Baldwin fails to account for the price changes that must accompany any gains from trade based on comparative advantage.[19] Baldwin's argument does, however, suggest that trade of this sort will surely produce additional dynamic gains for some countries of the world, and that therefore the global income increase in table 1–1 should be adjusted upward.

Again, however, it is hard to see that these dynamic effects, even if they were to double or to triple the welfare effects of the Uruguay Round, would alter the conclusion that these effects are not of overwhelming size. I therefore turn now to a discussion of whether there may be greater economic effects to be found in the parts of the agreement that have not been quantified.

Other Parts of the Uruguay Round

Much has been left out of the above analysis, as already noted. Most of us are confident that additional benefits from the round will result from the features listed in the bottom two-thirds of box 1–1. But how large will these benefits be? Nobody really knows the answer, and for most of these gains we do not even know how to frame the question. I expect these other gains to arise, however, and I believe they will constitute the important features of the round.

The new rules for safeguards, antidumping, and subsidies are far from perfect, but they do represent a step in the right direction. These rules are not intended to produce free trade, but rather to give governments constrained abilities to use policies to respond to market and political forces when necessary without having that process degenerate into a trade war. The rules will be successful if they are used (as the existing safeguards provision of the GATT is

---

18. Baldwin (1992).
19. Mazumdar (1994). The argument is that for countries that are exporters of capital goods, the gains from trade show up primarily as cheaper consumer goods and do not translate into any gain in investment.

not) and if they constrain governments from using these remedies excessively and capriciously. With some exceptions, the new rules in the Uruguay Round look as if they will accomplish this.

The most obvious gains from the "new issues"—TRIPSs, TRIMs, and services—are of the same kind as the gains from trade in goods, though they are much more difficult to quantify. Services trade itself is hard to measure, as are the barriers that interfere with it, but the motives for and gains from that trade are largely the same as for trade in goods. Curtailment of TRIMs, to the extent that they really are trade-related (constraining investors from importing, for example), will also have much the same effects as tariff removal. And the TRIPs agreement may also stimulate trade in those cases where firms have been reluctant to export because of fear that they would lose control over their intellectual property. So all of these new issues should add to the gains that the Uruguay Round will produce by reducing other barriers to trade.

It is easy to argue that the new issues will generate other gains that have nothing to do with trade. Greater openness in services is likely to mean an improved infrastructure in many countries, and this should facilitate economic activities of all sorts. TRIMs are of obvious importance in stimulating investment, so the dynamic effects here could be substantial. TRIPs have always been viewed as more important for stimulating innovation than for stimulating trade, and this too will be a source of dynamic gain.

Finally, the improved mechanism for settling disputes and the new WTO will both move the world one large step closer to an orderly international economic environment. Firms need to operate with confidence that they will not find their efforts undermined by governments acting only in their narrow national interests. These aspects of the Uruguay Round, if they work as well as hoped, improve this confidence and permit firms to respond to market forces rather than to the expectation or fear of government interference.

So I return, at the end, to the point with which I opened. In its most straightforward economic effects, the Uruguay Round is a positive but perhaps rather small move forward. But as a mechanism for reducing misguided government interference in markets and for signaling that countries are willing to accept market discipline, the Uruguay Round is critically important. It may not redirect the world economy onto a higher growth path, but it will permit the economic progress that has been achieved over the life of the GATT to be continued into the next century.

Comment by Thea M. Lee

This paper provides a sober and balanced overview of the economic literature on GATT, with a useful discussion of the likely broader benefits of the Uruguay Round and trade liberalization. The main theme is that the economic benefits and dislocations of GATT are shown in the literature to be fairly small. Deardorff argues, however, that the real value of the Uruguay Round lies in the more disciplined rules it imposes on the world trading system and the commitment it symbolizes on the part of governments to adhere to market principles and to forswear "self-destructive" interventions.

This conclusion—that the economic effects are small, but positive on net— is in keeping with a recently published International Trade Commission report. In surveying a similar group of studies, the ITC found that the likely economic gains from the Uruguay Round will be between 0.2 percent and 1 percent of U.S. GDP. This finding was reinforced by a qualitative industry-by-industry analysis.

While these survey findings (by Deardorff and the ITC) appear more reasonable than the inflated estimates currently being put forth by some GATT advocates, it is important to establish whether they represent a best-case scenario of well-functioning markets, including full employment and balanced trade, or a lower limit on possibly unmeasurable benefits. Deardorff takes the latter position. I would argue that there is room for discussion on this point.

As Deardorff notes, some of the transitional costs of trade liberalization are not calculated in the studies he reviewed. The paper provides estimates of gross labor market displacement and mentions (but does not quantify) several others: obsolete capital equipment, relocation costs for workers, and administrative costs for adjustment assistance programs. Having even rough estimates of these costs puts the magnitude of benefits in perspective.

In a paper such as this one, which summarizes a group of studies, it would be useful to know several things. First, what are the criteria used to choose the studies included? If any have been deliberately excluded, what are the reasons? Second, it would be helpful for the paper to provide closer scrutiny of the individual models: How and why do they differ in their structures? What accounts for the variability in their predictions? For example, they predict increases in global GDP growth ranging from 0.7 percent to 1.3 percent and expansion of global trade between 5 percent and 20 percent. Are all of these predictions equally plausible? These high-end predictions of the expansion of trade would seem to imply improbably high elasticities, given the fairly modest scale of tariff reductions.

While Deardorff makes a conscious attempt to achieve a balanced tone, the thrust of the paper nonetheless seems to be: Given that we know freer trade and freer markets are desirable, how can we strengthen the body of evidence to support this position? The problem with this stance is that it tends to bias the results, since the search for evidence and new models is all in the same direction.

Deardorff treats two classes of possible biases in the models he reviews—the failure to incorporate imperfect competition and increasing returns to scale and the failure to take into account the dynamic effects of trade liberalization. He argues that both of these omissions will lead to an underestimation of the gains from trade. It is possible, however, for both of these omissions to lead to overestimation as well.

Deardorff is mildly critical of the Harris-Cox model, which incorporates some elements of imperfect competition.[20] The model predicts gains from trade liberalization under the Canada-U.S. Free Trade Agreement (FTA) that are ten times higher than those of perfectly competitive models. Deardorff nonetheless cites this model as a plausible upper limit for measuring the results of taking imperfect competition into account. This, however, gives it too much credence, in my opinion, particularly given its poor predictive performance in the Canada-U.S. context.

The second model cited by Deardorff in this context, by Brown and Stern, assumed a monopolistically competitive market structure in the manufacturing sectors and found gains "only two or three times as large" as competitive models.[21] This model also was unable to predict consistently which sectors would expand and which would shrink after implementation of the FTA. Given the newness of this literature and the paucity of empirical support, it is too early to conclude on the basis of these models very much about the direction, let alone the magnitude of the gains, from trade not captured by competitive models. In fact, since the computable general equilibrium (CGE) models have deliberately incorporated imperfect competition only in ways that boost the size of the gains from trade, the results of these models demonstrate more about their sensitivity to small changes in assumptions than they do about reasonable upper limits on predicted gains.

---

20. Harris and Cox (1984).
21. Brown and Stern (1989).

It is also possible to argue—at least theoretically—that incorporating imperfect competition could reduce the estimated gains from trade. If there is concentration at the distribution level, then all the gains from trade will not necessarily be passed on to consumers dollar for dollar. This will affect the distribution of the gains from trade within the country, but not their magnitude. Second, to the extent that rational trade and investment agreements (like the North American Free Trade Agreement) favor multinational corporations over small- and medium-sized businesses, they could actually increase market concentration rather than boost competition. While this could increase economies of scale, it will also increase market power. The ultimate effect on price and efficiency is thus ambiguous. Similarly, increased protection of intellectual property rights (as is provided by both GATT and NAFTA) is also likely to strengthen monopoly power and raise consumer prices, especially in developing countries. None of these factors have yet been incorporated into CGE models. This could be an interesting area for future research.

Deardorff writes that economists began exploring the dynamic effects of trade when they found that static welfare gains measured by conventional CGE models were "disappointingly small." However, the evidence he cites in support of the idea that dynamic gains must necessarily be large relative to static gains is inconclusive. Rapid growth of the European Community or the Newly Industrializing Countries (NICs) in conjunction with trade liberalization could also be attributed to many other factors occurring concurrently, such as land reform or changes in labor market regulation.

There are several other possible sources of bias in the measurement of the gains from trade that Deardorff does not mention. The OECD model, for example, does not treat lost tariff revenues adequately. When tariffs are reduced, governments do not compensate by raising other taxes or reducing spending. In a global model with no leakages, this amounts to assuming that governments worldwide increase their deficit spending. The effect of this fiscal stimulus is magnified by multipliers. It would be interesting to see the effects of these models run with and without this feature to see how much difference it makes.

A second issue with the CGE models is the appropriateness of the full-employment assumption (equivalent to saying that the level of employment is determined solely by macroeconomic factors). Since the 1960s, the "natural" rate of unemployment has risen from less than 5 percent to more than 6 percent, with no single well-accepted explanation. If some portion of this increase is due to structural changes spurred by increased trade volumes (or lower trade barriers), then these models may not be capturing some of the labor-market effects of trade.

Finally, if we accept the basic conclusions of this paper, that the measurable economic effects of the Uruguay Round are "small" and that the symbolism and rules are more important, then we might also want to reopen discussion as to the nature of those rules and the openness of the mechanism for settling disputes.

Comment by Robert Lawrence

Alan Deardorff provides a cautious case for the Uruguay Round. He argues that in terms of its quantifiable economic effects the passage of the round's agreements will not make a big difference. Instead, he suggests that support for the round should be based on the fact that it represents one more step in the historic movement toward freer markets. Simply put, the Uruguay Round should be supported because it represents a small forward movement of the famous trade liberalization bicycle; it is really maintaining the forward momentum, rather than the specific movement the round will achieve, that is important. Deardorff's case for the round is that we had better keep pedaling to avoid falling backward. Indeed, for Deardorff, this particular turn of the wheels was not very impressive. According to him, this was a round that took an excessively long time to achieve some modest additional forward motion.

This is a useful paper, laying out the essential features of the agreement clearly and concisely and providing a good description and analysis of the literature estimating the round's quantitative effects. However, I would like to express two fundamental disagreements with Deardorff's characterization of its achievements. First, I believe the round's achievements are considerably more significant than he suggests; and second, I believe that its effects should be characterized as large rather than small.

Historic Significance

I think Deardorff fails to give adequate credit to what has been achieved in this agreement. It is the tone rather than the substance of his comments that I object to.

The Uruguay Round negotiations did last far longer than originally scheduled. Deardorff writes, "it is only the success of the system during the early postwar years that makes the current less rapid pace of economic growth appear a failure." Others have suggested that the delay indicates a failure of global leadership and the problems of dealing multilaterally when the numbers of participants proliferate. When the United States was a dominant hegemon, it would never have allowed this to happen.

But an alternative explanation of the time-consuming nature of the deliberations is that the goals and achievements of this negotiation were more ambitious than anything attempted before. Let me highlight six major examples:

—First, the inclusion of agriculture. It is noteworthy that, in the Kennedy Rounds, when the United States was the global hegemon, it was not able even to get agriculture on the agenda.

—Second, the introduction of new issues, such as services and intellectual property. When the United States proposed these issues in the early 1980s there was a great deal of skepticism both that these areas were important and that they should be included in the GATT.

—Third, the agreement to abolish the Multifiber Arrangement. Despite the fact that this agreement violated the essence of the GATT's principles—someone once likened the existence of the MFA in the GATT to the operation of a brothel in a cathedral—it remained a scourge on the system for more than thirty years. Yet it is now to be abolished.

—Fourth, the agreement to eliminate VRAs. What odds would a reasonable person have placed on achieving agreement about their abolition?

—Fifth, the enhanced status of the GATT as an institution and the increased power of its dispute settlement procedures. Until now, countries could refuse to accept findings; that is no longer an option.

—Sixth, the incorporation of all developing countries into all the GATT codes of behavior agreements. Previously, when it came to the codes only signatory countries were liable to their disciplines; now all GATT members are.

Finally, it is striking that the round dragged on, not because most countries disagreed, but rather because the two most important economies, those of the United States and the European Community, could not agree on one issue, agriculture. Once they did agree, it was astounding that this diverse group of nations could reach agreement on a vast range of issues. This should make us more optimistic about the possibilities of international agreement in the post-cold war era.

Of course, not all the U.S. goals were achieved. Nonetheless, it is clear that presidents of both parties have pushed very hard. It would be particularly inappropriate to reject what is here, because something else is not.

Size of Effects

I think Deardorff is simply wrong in characterizing the estimated effects as small and hardly worth the passage of the agreement. He reports estimates of the effects of the round that are in the range of a permanent increase of one percent of GNP, although he does note that the effects would be larger if more realistic modeling strategies were followed. Deardorff reminds me of the old joke in which a man is asked, "How's your wife?" and he replies, "Compared with what?" A key issue in how we appraise the Uruguay Round is compared with what? Deardorff argues its effects are small. But there are strong reasons to believe these estimates are lower bounds of the actual effects, and Deardorff is judging the round by the wrong comparators.

First, the effects are likely to be larger both because of the way the models have been constructed and because of what they neglect. As Deardorff notes, the one percent number comes from models that fail to account for scale economies, imperfect competition, and dynamic effects. Once these are taken into account, we know the effect will be considerably larger. Indeed, this is the central finding of David Richardson's survey from the OECD, and even Deardorff notes that "effects were only two or three times as large" if the model developed by Brown and others is correct, or "at most [sic] ten percent" if the Harris-Cox model is used.

I should also note that Deardorff would have obtained similar conclusions about all previous GATT agreements. The result that these agreements have "once and for all" effects is an assumption of the methodology of comparative statics rather than an empirical discovery.

Another reason for the limited size of these effects is that they do not cover all aspects of the agreement. Studies of the quantitative effects of trade measures resemble the proverbial drunk looking under the lamppost for his keys because that is where the light is. As Deardorff notes, only the reduction in tariffs and lowering of NTBs in agriculture and textiles are amenable to modeling.

Economic modeling is useful in capturing the effect of incremental change on a given economic system. It is far less able to capture the effects of changes in a legal order. Yet these changes can be extremely significant in affecting resource allocation. Insecurity about property rights for example acts as a severe tax on the incentive to invest. The concerns of the GATT have shifted away from incremental changes, which are readily modeled, toward changes in the rules of the game: defining property rights and permissible behavior by governments and firms. The quantitative estimates ignore the role of restraints on subsidies in preventing lobbying activities and the adoption of inefficient policies that would otherwise take place. Also overlooked is the contribution that more effective enforcement mechanisms will make in ensuring adherence to the rules.

Uncertainty is also given no weight in these models. In a conventional static model current tariff rates affect trade flows, and there is no room for the effects of policy uncertainty about future flows. Yet in the real world, these inter-temporal considerations and uncertainty can exert a crucial influence on invest-ment and trade flows. The conventional model therefore will give a zero weight to the remarkable fact that in the course of the Uruguay Round, according to Deardorff, developing countries have expanded the percentage of their imports covered by tariff bindings from 12 percent to more than half. (Deardorff does note potential but not quantified gains from TRIMs in stimulating investment and TRIPs in stimulating technology.)

Second, "compared with what." In my view a permanent increase of one percent of GNP is a large effect, not a small effect when compared with most other policy measures the U.S. Congress or other national leaders are ever likely to take. There are very few measures, in trade or in any policy area, that Congress can act on that can have a permanent effect on income of one percent of GNP. Moreover, these are benefits that come from using the same labor force and capital stock more efficiently and, aside from the costs of adjustment, involve no additional use of resources. Compared with comparable estimates of the models for the NAFTA, which did not incorporate scale economies, it is between fourteen and fifty times as large. Compare it with the "massive" budget package, which is estimated to have achieved a national savings of $500 billion over five years. If all of this saving were to be invested in an investment that yielded ten percent in perpetuity, it would yield $50 billion dollars, about one percent of GNP, and have roughly the same effect on real U.S. incomes. But that policy action requires five years of sacrificing consumption. This policy, by contrast, simply requires the one-time cost of adjusting resources. According to Deardorff this will involve about one percent of the labor force. Take an extreme example: Assume the cost of adjustment is half a year's pay. A one-time cost of half a percent then yields twice as much each year in perpetuity. Would you not invest 50 cents today to earn a dollar in perpetuity? In cost-benefit terms, this is a fantastic deal.

It is striking that the estimate of the "dislocation effects" are pretty small—about one month's change in employment in the recovery—and it is actually an overestimate because it ignores the ability to down-size through voluntary attrition and the possibility that there could be alternative reasons (for example, increases in domestic demand) for employment to change.

The modeling process that estimates the gains from the round uses the wrong benchmark. The counterfactual now is a world in which the round has been rejected rather than the world before the round's completion. In a strictly legal sense, rejection of the agreement would simply lead to the status quo. But this perspective would miss the blow to the momentum in liberalization that it would represent. It would be hard to underestimate the shock to the trading system that a failure of U.S. ratification would bring. The United States has served as the linchpin of the postwar trading order. It would be abrogating this position, something it did in the 1930s with disastrous consequences. It is hard to underestimate the importance of this measure to countries around the world, particularly the many developing countries. The ripple effects of trade frictions on financial markets has become a very strong factor in U.S.-Japan deliberations. The blow a rejection of the Uruguay Round would strike to global confidence would be quite similar.

Discussion

Much of the discussion focused on whether the models Deardorff discussed are adequate to capture the likely effects of the trade liberalization from the Uruguay Round Agreement. In particular, a number of conference participants believed that the static models in the paper underestimate the likely benefits, and they advocated more attention to dynamic modeling efforts. Warwick McKibbin referred to results from some of these efforts that imply significantly larger rises in global income through investment responses to anticipated productivity increases and to reductions in tariffs on capital goods. David Richardson noted that the role of international capital flows had been an important part of the debate over likely implications of NAFTA, and he advocated further assessment in this context as well.

Peter Wilcoxen raised concerns about how macroeconomic variables are treated in the general equilibrium trade models. For example, many of the models allow a country to run trade surpluses indefinitely, without incorporating the implied effects on asset accumulation, interest payments, or exchange rates. Similarly, Nancy Benjamin noted that simple rules, such as fixing the size of the current account, are often used to close these CGE models. While such rules can ensure that large capital movements do not swamp other effects, they are arbitrary and can significantly affect the results. Ralph Bryant seconded the concerns about closure rules and lack of attention to investment and to capital flows in the paper. However, he noted that existing dynamic models give a wide range of results, and he advocated further research to improve our understanding of them. David Walters mentioned that the administration has been talking about a dynamic gain in the range of 0.5 to 1.5 percent of GDP, in addition to the static gains of roughly 1 percent of GDP. While Robert Lawrence agreed that dynamics may be important, he disagreed with many previous speakers about the need to incorporate macroeconomic elements into the models. He argued that allowing the current account balance, employment, or other macroeconomic variables to adjust would confuse the results of modeling exercises designed to assess the implications of trade liberalization.

Walters cited work that suggests the degree of sectoral aggregation in many of the models may be a second reason to expect that existing studies underestimate the benefits from trade liberalization. He noted that most of the gains come from increased trade and efficiency as resources are reallocated among sectors. Little of this is captured, for example, in the OECD model, which groups 85 percent of U.S. manufacturing into a single sector. Deardorff raised a puzzle about aggregation, however. Although the Deardorff-Stern model is one of the most disaggregated, it implies one of the smallest gains. He agreed that sectoral aggregation is a critical aspect of model building and that additional work was needed to sort out this and other puzzles.

Barry Bosworth was surprised that so many participants were searching for reasons to scale up the estimates of the gains from liberalization. He argued there were as many reasons to expect these gains to be exaggerated. First, governments have considerable leeway to minimize the effects by choosing which tariffs to reduce. Second, he pointed out that empirical work on productivity has been unable to find large efficiency gains from intersectoral factor reallocations—the purported source of the GDP gains from trade liberalization.

He suggested studying past liberalizations to see if such an efficiency gain had in fact been realized.

Jagdish Bhagwati seconded the need for additional econometric work to pin down appropriate modeling assumptions for these efficiency gains as well as in other areas such as scale economies. More generally, he suggested that both empirical and theoretical work exploring channels that might reduce the gains from liberalization would be especially useful. However, Deardorff argued that we should not expect econometricians to be able to identify such efficiency gains in the data, given the relatively small effects the models suggest trade liberalization will have, compared with other shocks to the world economy over a multiyear period.

There was some discussion of the need for further disaggregation on the labor side, which Richardson pointed out had been important in the NAFTA debate. He noted that experiences are likely to vary across different types of workers—by skill level or wage, for example. Benjamin agreed that a better understanding of this would be useful. She referred to preliminary results from iterating between a trade model and the ITC's large, disaggregated model of the U.S. economy, which suggests smaller U.S. employment dislocations than those reported in table 1-1. Lewis Alexander also emphasized distributional issues, noting that the identifiability of clear losers is a key political issue. He stressed, however, that the employment dislocations must be kept in perspective. There is a large literature that attributes many worrisome recent trends, such as increased wage dispersion, to a variety of factors of which trade is a small part. Further, the likely flows are trivial compared with annual employment changes in the U.S. economy. There was some discussion of whether the labor market changes would be likely to occur gradually, and thus to get lost in the normal adjustment process. McKibbin argued that if the changes are credible, they should alter current behavior, so that Deardorff may have understated the short-run implications. However, Paul Wonnacott expressed concern that much of the liberalization has been put off to ease the pain. He argued that this may make the program less credible now and may entail a more painful adjustment in the future than if the liberalization had not been so heavily back-loaded.

There was also some discussion of the political problems raised by the fact that trade liberalization will reduce tariff revenues and thus have a negative effect on the budget. Alexander noted that the current budget rules do not incorporate any future economic consequences of a policy change because they were adopted to impose budgetary discipline. Thus the rules do not take into account future revenue increases as trade liberalization raises income. Bosworth argued that trade liberalization was merely one of a large number of worthwhile policies that should be expected to raise future productivity and that there was no more reason to exempt the trade agreement from current budget rules than to exempt day care, which is an investment in our children. In his view, the trade agreement is a tax reduction that should be offset by a tax increase in some other area. Wonnacott and Alexander expressed concern that any such tax increase could be explained to consumers as simply an offset.

Finally, Catherine Mann discussed potential implications for future trade negotiations of the two-pronged nature of the Uruguay Round Agreement. She hypothesized that the two tracks might become more distinct, with traditional liberalization efforts undertaken among smaller country groups, while multilateral negotiations focused on rules and disciplines. Thea Lee argued that it may be difficult to separate the two tracks, noting that compromises across issue areas were essential for reaching agreement in the past round.

References

Baldwin, Richard E. 1992. "Measurable Dynamic Gains from Trade." *Journal of Political Economy* 100: 162–74.

Brown, Drusilla K., Alan V. Deardorff, and Robert M. Stern. 1992. "A U.S.-Mexico-Canada Free Trade Agreement: Sectoral Employment Effects and Regional/Occupational Employment Realignments in the United States." In National Commission for Employment Policy, *The Employment Effects of the North American Free Trade Agreement: Recommendations and Background Studies*, Special Report, October.

Brown, Drusilla K., and Robert M. Stern. 1989. "U.S.-Canada Bilateral Tariff Elimination: The Role of Product Differentiation and Market Structure." In Robert C. Feenstra, ed., *Trade Policies for International Competitiveness*. University of Chicago Press.

Burniaux, J. M., J. P. Martin, F. Delorme, I. Leinert, and D. van der Mensbrugghe. 1990. "Economy-Wide Effects of Agricultural Policies in OECD Countries: A GE Approach Using the Walras Model." In I. Goldin and O. Knudsen, eds., *Agricultural Trade Liberalization*. Paris: OECD and the World Bank.

Deardorff, Alan V., and Robert M. Stern. 1990. *Computational Analysis of Global Trading Arrangements*. University of Michigan Press.

Francois, Joseph, Bradley McDonald, and Håkan Nordström. 1993. "Economywide Effects of the Uruguay Round," GATT Background Paper, December 3.

Goldin, I., O. Knudsen, and D. van der Mansbrugghe. 1993. *Trade Liberalisation: Global Economic Implications*. Paris: OECD and the World Bank.

Grossman, Gene M., and Elhanan Helpman. 1991. *Innovation and Growth in the Global Economy*. MIT Press.

Harris, Richard G., and David Cox. 1984. *Trade, Industrial Policy, and Canadian Manufacturing*. Toronto: Ontario Economic Council.

Jackson, John H. 1989. *The World Trading System*. MIT Press.

Lucas, Robert E., Jr. 1988. "On the Mechanics of Economic Development." *Journal of Monetary Economics* 22: 3–42.

Mazumdar, Joy. 1994. "Do Static Gains from Trade Lead to Medium Run Growth?" mimeo, University of Michigan.

Nguyen, Trien T., Carlo Perroni, and Randall M. Wigle. 1991. "The Value of a Uruguay Round Success." *The World Economy* 14: 359–74.

Nguyen, Trien T., Carlo Perroni, and Randall M. Wigle. 1993. "An Evaluation of the Draft Final Act of the Uruguay Round." *Economic Journal* 103: 1540–49.

OECD. 1993. "Assessing the Effects of the Uruguay Round." Mimeo. Paris: OECD.

Romer, Paul M. 1986. "Increasing Returns and Long-Run Growth." *Journal of Political Economy* 94: 1002–37.

Agriculture and
Natural Resources

Tim Josling

Agriculture, as is well known, was among the most difficult issues facing the trade negotiators in the Uruguay Round. Disagreement on the modalities of negotiation in agriculture caused the Montreal Mid-term Meeting to be adjourned in December 1988, causing the round to lose momentum. Again, at the final meeting in December 1990, the negotiations on agriculture held up progress on a package, though other aspects of the negotiations were probably also not ready to be concluded. Agricultural talks consumed most of 1991 and 1992 before the United States and the European Union reached an agreement, and even then this Blair House Accord almost came unraveled in 1993. The problems of agriculture will not subside just because agreement has been reached. The World Trade Organization (WTO), which was set up to administer the Uruguay Round outcome and to take over the functions of the GATT, will have as one of its most difficult tasks the implementation of an ambitious and wide-ranging Agreement on Agriculture.

This agreement attempts to bring agriculture under the full disciplines of international trade rules by a three-pronged attack on the existing trade distortions. It mandates the conversion of all nontariff import measures to bound

The author is Professor of Economics at the Food Research Institute, Stanford University. The paper has benefited from the comments of the participants at the Brookings Institution Conference. A more detailed paper on the same subject has been prepared for the International Agricultural Trade Research Consortium. A paper by Tangermann deals with the more technical aspects of implementing the agreement.[1]

1. Josling and others (1994). Tangermann (1994).

tariffs; it sets a limit on existing export subsidies and prohibits new export subsidies; and it gives an incentive to countries to move to less trade-distorting domestic support systems. In addition it shelters some aspects of national farm policies from GATT challenges and lays down less restrictive schedules for developing countries. In a related agreement, new rules for the setting of sanitary and phytosanitary standards have been established. These are designed to make it more difficult for countries to use such standards as trade barriers.

Was it all worthwhile? Has the agreement made a significant improvement to the trade system? Or did agriculture manage to escape once more from the disciplines of agreed trade rules? This paper is an attempt to evaluate the agreement as it relates to the trade system for agricultural products and to the development of more rational farm policies. The conclusion will be that the agreement does indeed put in place a new set of rules that could lead to an improved trade system for agriculture. This conclusion should be qualified by the realization that not much actual liberalization was agreed on in agricultural markets and that much depends on the will and actions of governments to make the agreement work. If the agreement is used as a first stage in a continuing process of tariff reduction and subsidy restraint, it will have proved path-breaking. If it becomes an object of neglect and evasion, and if governments are obliged to reverse recent liberal reforms of farm policies, then all the effort will have been for naught.

The emphasis placed on agriculture in the Uruguay Round of trade negotiations emanated from a number of quarters. In part it stemmed from those countries that saw closed markets and restricted trade opportunities as anomalous with the more liberal trade regime in manufactured goods. In part it stemmed from frustration that rules for agricultural trade were not precise enough to be useful either in preventing disputes or in resolving disputes once they had arisen. But the main emphasis came from a widespread sense that the systems of domestic farm support in industrial countries had become too costly and troublesome, that these programs were in large part responsible for the chaos in world agricultural trade, and that an international solution to these domestic problems was possible through modified trade rules and an agreement to lower protection. This link with national policies set the Uruguay Round talks on agriculture apart from previous rounds of trade negotiations. It is also the factor that made the negotiations so prolonged and the final agreement so difficult to reach.

Unlike many areas of trade policy, it was never easy to separate the issue of agricultural trade rules from the conduct of domestic farm policy. Given the political strength of groups that had a stake in these domestic policies, trade policy tended to take a back seat. Had the issue not been tackled in the Uruguay Round, any resulting trade agreement would have been of doubtful value. Among the main issues in evaluating the outcome of the round are therefore the extent to which domestic agricultural policy reforms are encouraged by the negotiations and the extent to which these policies are effectively constrained by the terms of the agreement.

Agriculture had hardly been ignored in earlier rounds of GATT negotiations. The Dillon Round, not particularly successful in other respects, had included a deal between the European Community (EC) and the United States to bind at a zero or low duty a number of "minor" products, such as soybeans, high-protein meals, and cassava. These items became among the fastest growing items in trade with the EC. The Kennedy Round had made a serious effort to tackle agricultural issues, but had in the end settled for an international agreement on wheat (the International Grains Arrangement), which collapsed shortly after the end of the round. In the Tokyo Round, agricultural trade had benefited a little from the reduction of some quantitative trade restrictions, notably by Japan, but no substantive degree of liberalization had been possible. The two commodity agreements concluded in the Tokyo Round, for dairy products and for beef, were of little long-term value as ways of liberalizing trade. It had not proved possible to reach an agreement on the international management of grain stocks. With high agricultural prices on world markets at the start of the Tokyo Round in 1974, market liberalization appeared less pressing than stabilization. None of these rounds had tried to deal effectively with the causes of agricultural trade problems.

World agricultural markets were again firm in the period after the Tokyo Round, with the United States experiencing record agricultural export earnings in 1981. Against this backdrop, the early plans for agriculture in the upcoming round focused on rule changes to assist the settlement of disputes. A GATT Committee on Agriculture was appointed in 1982 to look at such rule changes. By 1986 the situation had changed dramatically. World prices were on a downward slide, reaching their lowest point for many years. U.S. agricultural exports fell precipitously, and support costs escalated. Export subsidy programs were reintroduced, and trade disputes became more common and more bitter. In the European Community subsidized exports became the main outlet for surplus production, at an increasingly high cost. Small and medium-sized exporters of agricultural goods began increasingly to suffer under the burden of the export market competition of the two agricultural "super powers." In this situation, the prospect of the Uruguay Round as a solution to the disarray in world markets began to look more attractive. By the time governments met in Punta del Este to launch the Uruguay Round of trade negotiations, a general consensus had been reached that it was necessary to reform agricultural policies in order to achieve trade liberalization in agriculture.

The Uruguay Round Negotiations on Agriculture

The Uruguay Round negotiations on agriculture fall conveniently into three phases. In the first phase countries exchanged ideas as to the approach to be taken to improving agricultural trade and the way in which negotiations should proceed. This phase began in September 1986, after the launch of the round at Punta del Este. In July 1987, the United States unveiled its dramatic proposal for eliminating all trade-distorting farm programs over a ten-year period. All that would be left would be "decoupled" payments—those not tied to output—together with genuine food aid and domestic nutrition and poverty programs. As a mechanism to be used to embody these commitments the OECD PSE (producer subsidy equivalents) measure was suggested, which aggregated the effects of diverse policy instruments into a subsidy equivalent. The newly formed Cairns Group, fourteen small and medium-sized agricultural exporters, followed with a proposal that would entail an immediate freeze on price supports followed by a phased reduction, until finally a new set of rules could be introduced to regulate agricultural trade. The EC countered with a two-part proposal to negotiate reductions in support levels, but only after action in the short run to shore up world prices.

This first phase produced more heat than light, and it culminated in the collapse of the negotiations at a meeting in Montreal in December 1988. The Cairns Group insisted on progress in agriculture before the talks could proceed. The EC and the United States could not agree on the scope and objective of the negotiations nor the modalities to be used. The talks were rescued in April 1989, when countries finally agreed to a "midterm" package of measures, laying down a freeze in support prices (the first time such an agreement had been possible) and indicating the timetable for the rest of the negotiations. More significantly, the package included a political commitment to a progressive reduction in trade-distorting subsidies, to the improvement of import access, and to the curbing of export subsidies.

The second phase of the negotiations comprised an elaboration of the negotiating ideas by each (major) participant, with the intention of leading to a common document on which all parties could focus attention. At this stage the form of the final agreement began to take shape. The United States proposed an approach that, in contrast to its original paper of 1987, would focus on rules to guide both domestic policies and trade in agricultural products. Nontariff import barriers were to be converted into tariffs. Export subsidies were to be banned. Domestic policies were to be categorized into those that were acceptable, that is, minimally trade-distorting; those that were objectionable and therefore had to be reduced; and those that should be prohibited. The Cairns Group broadly supported this approach. The EC, however, argued against the imposition of rules on the use of individual policy instruments. Though the community reluctantly agreed to a form of tariffication, it resisted strongly the control of export subsidies. In place of the "rules" approach, the EC argued for an across-the-board cut in support levels by means of an instrument similar to that proposed by the United States in 1987.

In June 1990, the chairman of the Negotiating Group on Agriculture, Aart de Zeeuw, attempted to pull all of these ideas together in a single negotiating document. This paper (the Chairman's Draft) presented a blueprint for a substantial and comprehensive draft agreement, but it still did not command full support as "a basis for negotiations." The EC felt that it followed too closely the U.S./Cairns Group line and rejected it. Despite further attempts to get consensus, the "final" negotiations in Brussels in December 1990 collapsed, largely as a result of the impasse on agriculture. Once again, the Cairns Group indicated its unwillingness to settle for a weak compromise on agriculture. Agreement on the structure of an agricultural package did not occur until February 1991, after the EC had proposed substantial modifications in its own internal agricultural policy so as to be able to live with the changes implied by a GATT agreement.

The third and final phase of the negotiations was to develop the details of such an agreement as it would apply to all the participating countries. These details were incorporated into the "Draft Final Act" of December 1991, submitted by Arthur Dunkel, the director general of the GATT, and usually called the Dunkel Draft. The Dunkel Draft kept the tripartite structure of "market access," "export competition," and "domestic support" and introduced the timetable for liberalization of support and protection. The Dunkel Draft was modified somewhat by the Blair House Accord, in November 1992, between the United States and the EC, and later refined by the last-minute negotiations in Geneva in December 1993. But the main elements of the Dunkel Draft have found their way into the Agreement on Agriculture. The time between the end of the negotiations in Geneva and the signing of the Final Act in Marrakesh was devoted to a clarification and verification of the individual schedules that compose the details of the implementation of the agreement.

The Provisions

The terms of the Agreement on Agriculture (hereafter the Agreement) are contained in Annex 1A, the Agreement on Trade in Goods, to the Agreement Establishing the World Trade Organization.[2] Important detail covering implementation of the Agreement on Agriculture is contained in the commitments entered into by each individual country in schedules that form part of the overall agreement. Scrutiny of the full schedules will take some time. In the meantime, judgment must be based on the articles of the Agreement and on the schedules for the larger countries, which have become generally available.

The most important aspect of the Agreement is that it establishes a set of completely new and operational rules for agriculture. In particular, it results in a legally effective binding of tariff rates for agricultural goods and imposes constraints on the most trade-distorting types of agricultural policies used throughout the world. This fact in itself is a radical departure from the way in which agriculture is treated in the GATT. Formerly, governments had much scope to design and to pursue their agricultural policies as they saw fit for their domestic interests and to treat agriculture as a special case under trade rules. As a result, the GATT did not effectively constrain most government actions in agriculture that affect trade. After the Uruguay Round, governments will have to observe binding commitments (bindings) that they have accepted under international law. These bindings cover nearly all border measures, both on the import and on the export side, and they also apply to the total of trade-distorting domestic support, to the extent that it has a noticeable effect on international trade. It is hard to overestimate the significance of this fundamental change. An important sector in world trade, which has escaped most GATT disciplines since the inception of the General Agreement, is now for the first time effectively brought under control.

---

2. This discussion of the terms of the Agreement draws heavily on the more extensive description in Josling and others (1994).

The effectiveness of the Agreement is enhanced not only by the general rules that it establishes for agricultural trade, but also by the specific commitments all participating countries undertake, which are expressed in their schedules. The real power of the Agreement lies in the binding nature of these country-specific commitments, because they relieve the process of implementing the Agreement from much of the need to find appropriate interpretations of general rules for each individual policy of each individual country. Indeed, all waivers and special exemptions for agriculture in the trade rules are to be removed. New types of commitments have been made that did not exist previously in the GATT, either in agriculture or in other sectors. Whereas GATT schedules in the past contained only tariff bindings, their agricultural components now also contain bindings regarding export subsidies and total support. This legal innovation is an important aspect of the agricultural negotiations, necessitated by the complexity of dealing with domestic farm policies at the international level.

The Agreement on Agriculture is best understood by taking separately the three major areas on which negotiations focused—import access, export competition, and domestic support. In each of these three areas, two approaches were applied: the definition of new rules and the reduction in levels of support and protection. Each substantive area includes a set of safeguards, qualifications, accommodations, and guarantees necessary for reaching the agreement. The provisions of the Agreement apply less stringently to developing countries under the principle of "Special and Differential Treatment," and the negotiators agreed that special measures might have to be taken if world price increases had a particularly severe effect on food-importing developing countries.

Market Access

The market access provisions are notable for two rule changes:

—nontariff border measures are to be converted to tariffs
—all tariffs are to be bound (they cannot be increased without negotiation with trading partners)

This is perhaps the most far-reaching element in the Agreement. The changes take effect immediately. With very few exceptions, all participating countries have agreed to convert all existing nontariff barriers (along with unbound tariffs) into bound duties from the date of entry into force of the Agreement, and not to introduce new nontariff measures (article 4 of the Agreement). Along with the existing tariffs, these new tariffs will have to be reduced according to schedules. The reductions embodied in the schedules were based on the following guidelines:[3]

—target reduction of tariffs 36 percent (on average) over 6 years from a 1986–88 base
—minimum reduction of 15 percent per tariff line

Developing countries were allowed to reduce tariffs at a slower rate, namely:

—reduction of 24 percent (on average) over ten years

In order to make tariffication acceptable to importers, special safeguards were included for specified imports, in the event of import surges and low world prices (article 5).

—for products subject to tariffication, additional duties (up to one-third of normal duties) can be levied for the remainder of the market year if imports exceed a certain percentage of the preceding three-year average, called the "trigger" level of imports[4]
—alternatively, additional duties can be levied for these products if world prices fall below preset "trigger" price levels, on a sliding scale relating to the difference between the import price and the trigger price.

To guard against loss of market access in the process of tariffication and to secure visible medium-term trade gains, the agreement provides in cases of tariffication for "minimum access opportunities" as follows:

—import opportunities to be granted for a share of domestic consumption (generally 3 percent, rising to 5 percent) by means of a reduced tariff quota,
—current access opportunities (for example under quotas and voluntary export restraint agreements) to be maintained at the 1986–88 level.

---

3. The target commitments participating countries were expected to make in their schedules were not included in the text of the Agreement, but in a separate document entitled "Modalities for the Establishment of Specific Binding Commitments under the Reform Programme." This document has lost its legal power now that the schedules have been accepted.

4. The trigger level is set at 105 percent of base period imports for those products where imports are more than 30 percent of the domestic market; at 110 percent of base imports where imports compose between 10 and 30 percent of consumption; and at 125 percent where imports account for less than 10 percent of domestic sales. The trigger level is, then, adjusted by the change in domestic consumption between the two most recent years, but it cannot drop below 105 percent of the preceding three-year average.

The agreement to convert all nontariff import barriers to bound tariffs takes agricultural trade a big step toward the same treatment as manufactures within the GATT. Tariffication has a number of desirable features, including greater transparency of trade measures, for both the traders and the domestic interests influenced by tariffs; the removal of a number of "grey-area" techniques used by countries to control imports, such as variable levies, which effectively escaped GATT disciplines; the ease of binding and subsequent reduction of tariffs; the improved distribution among countries of the burden of adjustment to world market shocks; the greater influence of market signals in shaping production and consumption decisions; and the indirect control of the level of export subsidies implied by the absence of nontariff barriers to reimporting. Over time tariffication will change the nature of world trade in agricultural goods, leading to more liberal, more predictable, and more stable world markets.

However, the process of improving market access conditions through tariffication was not complete and unconditional. Because of the domestic difficulties Japan and Korea had with the prospect of opening up their rice markets, a special treatment clause was included in the Agreement (annex 5). Under conditions tailored to the two cases concerned, this clause allows those two countries a delay of tariffication for at least a few years.

Export Competition

The ability of trade rules to define and control export subsidies in agriculture was one of the main issues under discussion in the negotiation. The Agreement attempts for the first time to establish the level of such subsidies deemed to exist in the base period. This leads to a significant new rule:

—no new export subsidies (other than those notified in the schedules) can be introduced.

Existing export subsidies are subject to reduction disciplines, as follows:

—budget expenditures on export subsidies are to be reduced by 36 percent over six years, from 1986–90 levels, in each of twenty-two product categories

—the volume of subsidized exports is to be reduced by 21 percent over six years from 1986–90, in each of twenty-two product categories.[5]

---

5. There are, of course, no reductions required on nonsubsidized exports.

Once more, developing countries have to undertake only two-thirds of the reduction, in a longer time period:

—developing countries need only reduce expenditure by 24 percent over ten years; developing countries need only reduce volume by 14 percent over ten years.

To ensure that developing country importers do not get disadvantaged, "genuine" food aid is exempt from reductions.

An attempt was also made to define more clearly what constitutes an export subsidy. Such subsidies are deemed to be payments in kind; subsidized stock exports; producer-financed export subsidies; export marketing cost subsidies; export-specific transportation subsidies; and subsidies on goods incorporated into exports.[6]

Members have entered base levels of subsidized exports and of outlays on export subsidies into their schedules, agreeing that the figures contained in the schedules are an accurate representation of their export subsidization in the past. More important, based on these past levels of export subsidization, countries have individually accepted legally binding commitments regarding maximum export subsidization in the future (article 3). Hence, for the first time in the history of the GATT there can no longer be any doubts as to what (maximum) level of export subsidies a country can grant in agricultural trade.

To define export subsidies clearly, the Agreement contains a list of such subsidies falling under schedule commitments (article 9). Moreover, there are provisions guarding against circumvention of commitments, including rules on food aid (article 10). The burden of proof for not subsidizing exports is laid on the exporting country (article 10:3). In addition, there is agreement not to extend export subsidies to commodities not subsidized in the base period (article 3:3 and Modalities, paragraph 12).[7] To provide some flexibility, countries can shift their export subsidy commitments between individual years of

---

6. Export credits and credit guarantees are to be covered by a separate agreement.

7. Paragraph 12 of the Modalities also provides for the possibility of negotiating commitments regarding exports to individual or regional markets. Where such commitments were agreed, they should have been specified in the schedules. It appears that this has not happened anywhere. This does not, however, mean that there are no bilateral agreements of this nature that have been kept outside the GATT legal framework (an example is the "Andriessen commitment" regarding EC beef exports to the Pacific Rim).

the implementation period, though only within narrowly defined limits (article 9:2(b)).

Domestic Support

Another innovative feature of the Agreement is the set of rules and commitments it establishes for domestic support policies, through in practice the influence of this innovation is likely to be modest. Given the importance of the link between domestic agricultural policies and international trade, the fact that GATT commitments now impose quantitative constraints on certain types of domestic support is itself significant.

The main rule change in the case of domestic support is to define:

—policies fulfilling certain "green box" criteria, which are deemed to be minimally trade-distorting (research, extension, inspection, marketing and promotion, infrastructure; food security stocks, domestic food aid, crop insurance, income safety-net schemes, disaster payments, retirement programs, set-asides, structural adjustment programs, environmental programs; "decoupled" income support).

For developing countries the list is extended to include

—rural development programs, investment subsidies, input subsidies, and diversification subsidies.

Payments for policies other than "green box" measures are subject to reduction, as follows:

—reduction in total trade distorting domestic support, aggregated across all commodities, of 20 percent in six years, from a 1986–88 base.

However, a major breach in the integrity of the "green box" notion was introduced by excluding from the reduction commitments:

—direct payments under production-limiting programs not subject to reduction if they are based on fixed area and yields; made on 85 percent or less of base production; and livestock payments made on a fixed number of head.

The nature of these constraints warrants some explanation. The variable constrained under the "domestic support" commitments is not just expenditure on domestic subsidies, but the level of total support (including market price support through administered prices) provided by policies covered under the Agreement. This support includes an element of market price support, measured against fixed external reference prices of the base period. This together with the expenditure on included domestic programs becomes the Aggregate Measurement of Support (AMS). The AMS is aggregated over both policy instruments and commodities. The Agreement specifies the method of calculation of the AMS (annex 3), requires countries to enter their base period (1986–88) AMS in their schedules (article 1(a)(i)), and sets the rate of reduction of 20 percent over the six-year implementation period, resulting in annual AMS commitments specified in the schedules (Modalities, paragraph 8).

In order to encourage a shift of policies, measures "with no, or at most minimal, trade distortion effects or effects on production" have been exempted from reduction commitments under the AMS approach. This "green box" is defined in both general form and in a list of eligible policies. As a result of the Blair House Accord between the United States and the EC, another exemption was agreed. It was decided that neither the U.S. deficiency payments nor the new compensation payments under the reformed Common Agricultural Policy of the EC need to be included in the AMS calculation. In this way, both the United States and the EC escape the reduction commitment on major aspects of their domestic policy. Another important consequence of the Blair House Accord was the decision to make domestic support commitments not product-specific but sector-wide (article 6:1).

Sanitary and Phytosanitary Measures

Participants also concluded an Agreement on Sanitary and Phytosanitary Measures (the SPS Agreement).[8] The goal was to improve on the present operation of article XX by making it easier to distinguish between genuine health and safety issues and disguised protection. The right of countries to set their own safety and health standards is reaffirmed, but with the proviso that such standards should be based on "scientific justification" and that use be made of international standards where possible.

Although the SPS Agreement is separate from the Agreement on Agriculture, it has close substantive links with it. In particular, commitments to reduce economic barriers to trade may reinforce tendencies to use technical standards

---

8. For a more detailed treatment of this topic see Tangermann (1994), on which the present discussion is based.

to provide protection to domestic farmers. But in addition to guarding against such inappropriate use of sanitary and phytosanitary standards, there are also many "technical" issues relating to such standards in their own right that needed to be better regulated at the international level. In particular, it was important to make sure that these standards can achieve their objectives in the protection of human, animal, and plant life and health, while not resulting in economic waste by creating undue restrictions on international trade.

The SPS Agreement is an impressive step in this direction, and it has the potential of proving as important in its area as the Agreement on Agriculture in the realm of economic measures. It is therefore appropriate to think of the new rules regarding SPS as the fourth pillar of the Uruguay Round achievements in the area of agriculture, complementing effectively the new rules and commitments in the three areas of market access, export competition, and domestic support.

The character of the SPS Agreement is rather different from the Agreement on Agriculture. In particular, the SPS Agreement does not attempt to regulate any specific policies. Hence, individual countries are not committed to make adjustments in their policies. The SPS Agreement instead establishes general guidelines for government behavior in the areas concerned. Some of these guidelines are open to interpretation. It is therefore not directly evident which measures in which countries will have to change in which ways. Consequently it is difficult to spell out in any detail the implications of this Agreement for trade flows and price levels on international markets. Much will depend on the spirit in which governments implement their measures under the new guidelines.

Implementation will rely heavily on the two principles of harmonization and equivalence laid down in the SPS Agreement. Where harmonization is achieved—where national SPS are based on standards agreed in the relevant international institutions—policies are presumed to be consistent with the Agreement and the GATT, and disputes should not arise. Nevertheless, harmonization at the international level may not always be appropriate. The Agreement therefore allows the alternative of equivalence, whereby the importing country accepts that the SPS in the exporting country can achieve an appropriate level of sanitary or phytosanitary protection, even though they differ from the measures used in the importing country. Indeed, widespread application of the equivalence principle may in the longer run implicitly result in growing harmonization as trading partners learn more about each other's measures and find out which measures are most appropriate in which cases.

Where a country does not rely on harmonization or equivalence, but rather insists on its own domestic standards, it must comply with a number of requirements. It must ensure that its measures do not discriminate between countries where identical or similar conditions prevail, and it must not apply them as a disguised restriction on international trade. These requirements are fundamentally those that have always existed under GATT article XX, except that they are now somewhat more demanding.[9] However, there is now also the requirement to ensure that the measures concerned are consistent with scientific evidence and that they are based on an appropriate risk assessment. These additional requirements are completely new in the GATT, and governments will have to develop suitable procedures for fulfilling them.

The test of "scientific justification" is a general rule, which is likely to be crucial to the implementation of the SPS Agreement. It is not without ambiguity, however. There will be cases in which scientists disagree on the precise implications of particular practices (for example, the effect on human health of a hormone fed to livestock destined for human consumption). There may also be disagreement on the level of risk from which protection should be provided. The SPS Agreement has a number of detailed provisions on appropriate risk assessment, but again by their very nature they can only be general and therefore must leave scope for interpretation in each individual case. Much will therefore depend on the speed, vigor, and effectiveness of settling disputes that may arise from inconsistent interpretations of the relevant Agreement provisions. Accordingly, a new WTO Committee on Sanitary and Phytosanitary Measures is to be established under the Agreement.

Although many view the new SPS Agreement as a significant advance, it is difficult to say how effective it will be in curbing trade disputes arising from health and safety standards. It could also lead to unwarranted changes in such standards. Many environmental and consumer groups fear that there will be an erosion of standards in the name of freer trade. The significance of these trade rules may soon be apparent. There are many important issues, such as inconsistent regulations on the use of Bovine Somatotropin in dairy production, different approaches to food irradiation, and disparate requirements for food labeling that threaten to burst on the trade scene, testing these new SPS procedures.

---

9. Not only identical, but also similar conditions must be honored; no discrimination "between countries" now explicitly includes its own territory for the country applying the SPS.

The "Peace Clause"

As an incentive for countries to accept the new disciplines and commitments on domestic support and export subsidies, it was agreed that policies that conform to the new rules are sheltered from international challenge under the GATT. The Due Restraint provisions (article 13), valid during the implementation period, state that "green box" policies (in accordance with annex 2 of the Agreement) are nonactionable for purposes of countervailing duties and other GATT challenges; all domestic support that conforms with commitments, including payments under production-limiting programs (U.S. deficiency payments and EC compensation payments), is exempt from the imposition of countervailing duties as long as it does not cause injury and is exempt from other GATT challenges as long as support does not exceed that paid in 1992; and export subsidies within the constraints of the Agreement are exempt from most GATT challenge and subject to countervailing duties only if they cause injury.

The Uruguay GATT Round offers to improve trade relations in agriculture in no small part by improving bilateral relations between countries, notably the United States and the European Union (EU). Such agricultural trade conflicts will not disappear overnight, but they will take place within a clearer framework of rules and obligations. This attractive scenario could be enough to change national policy behavior. By constraining agricultural policies within effective GATT rules, countries would incur much greater risks with policies that offer excessive protection to agriculture. National policies will run up against these constraints and adapt more quickly.

Evaluation of the Agreement

Evaluation of the Agreement requires some subjective judgments on the behavior of governments and the future trends in economic policy. It is possible to build a case that emphasizes the significant progress that has been made in bringing agriculture under "more effective rules and disciplines." It is also possible to emphasize the lack of trade liberalization that is imposed by the modest cuts in support levels. These two views are not factually inconsistent; they merely emphasize different features of the Agreement. Like a glass both half-full and half-empty, they give scope for alternative scenarios of the future. Can the glass be filled further in future negotiations, or will the liquid spill and the glass soon be empty again? These two scenarios lead to very different conclusions about the future of agricultural trade relations.

The "half-full" argument puts faith in the establishment of new rules. The Agreement on Agriculture, if ratified, would constitute a major step toward the effective establishment of an improved set of rules for agricultural trade. The chances of these rules being effectively enforced through the dispute settlement mechanism are also increased. The rules that impose tariffs as the only allowed border protection are clear and relatively unequivocal. With the exceptions of Japan and Korea and a few other countries that matched the criteria for the "rice clause," tariffs will become the only allowable border regime for agriculture. This could plausibly lead to a future dominated by active negotiations on tariff reduction, as a part of a new multilateral round, as a component in regional trade liberalization, or as a result of pressure from food processors and consumers to remove high protection levels. The agreement not to introduce new export subsidies, combined with the need to reduce both expenditure on and quantity of presently subsidized exports, removes much of the threat of a return to the price wars of the mid-1980s. Allowing countries to redesign domestic policies to escape challenge and countervail, and to escape inclusion in the Aggregate Measure of Support, should also help to reduce trade tensions.

Finally, the SPS Agreement could be seen as holding out the hope for a firm basis for distinguishing between sensible and protectionist use of standards-related trade measures. Under this interpretation, the Agreement is so clearly a major step forward that to downplay it is to risk perpetuating the gloom often surrounding the topic and reinforcing the mind-set that denies that constructive international action is possible.

The "half-empty" argument acknowledges the significance of the principle of tariffication, but points to the way in which it was done as being an indication of the true intent of governments. Some significant slippage occurred in moving from tariffication at the previous levels (corresponding to the nontariff trade measures that the tariffs were to replace) to the initial tariffs to be inserted in the Schedule. Many countries produced "offers" for tariffication that built in the scope for more protection in the short run.[10] Others chose to take full advantage of the fact that the guidelines only asked for an unweighted average reduction of tariffs by 36 percent. The negotiations that took place on the basis of these offers seem not to have succeeded in reducing either the height of the new tariffs or the reduction rates. Instead, countries appear to have concentrated on the distribution of the minimum access quantities in the form

---

10. For a partial exploration of the way in which countries took advantage of tariffication to raise protection, see Josling and Tangermann (1994).

of a set of bilateral side-deals. The result is arguably a complex set of trade relations bearing little resemblance to a straight most favored nation tariff regime.

This interpretation of the outcome as business as usual in agricultural trade politics also emphasizes the minimal effect the Agreement will have on the major participants, such as the United States, the EU, and Japan. The United States and the EU were able to strike the bargain that removed the payments under their respective cereals programs from the discipline of reduction. The EU was forced, in effect, to keep its variable levy for grains as a result of a "maximum duty-paid import price" provision set at the level of the current threshold price. Neither the United States nor the EU are likely soon to be near the constraint imposed on domestic support or on export subsidy expenditure. A last-minute modification to the Blair House Accord took much of the near-term pressure off the EU and the United States in the area of export subsidy quantity reduction. Japan was let off the hook with respect to rice policy liberalization, even though the poor rice harvest had led to considerable imports of rice this year.

The pessimism of the "half-empty" argument places little reliance on the fact that a process has been started that will pay off in the future. The optimism of the "half-full" argument ignores the fact that degree of protection in the agricultural trade system is itself a problem that causes friction and puts all rules in jeopardy.[11] The reconciliation between the two points of view would therefore seem to hinge on whether countries will continue in the way that has characterized the past decade, toward lower support prices, less state intervention in marketing, and severe budget reductions for farm programs that do not have strong political support. If such a trend were to continue, one could see the next mini-round on agriculture being a constructive consolidation of gains made so far, with further (formula-based) reductions in tariffs, further mandated cuts in export subsidy expenditure, and a move to tighten the "green box" in particular to bring the U.S. and EU crop payments under its discipline. This scenario also presupposes that countries that have built some slack into their new tariffs do not exploit this opportunity to raise trade barriers.

---

11. One lesson that should have been learned from the management of domestic farm policies over the past forty years is that any type of market price policy is easy to administer if price levels are not set too high, but that no type of policy device will be satisfactory if the price levels are excessive.

By contrast, the prospects for trade if countries were to revert to more protection is cloudy. The problem in this case might be that the rules are not themselves tight enough to prevent such recidivism. The level of bound tariffs, even when reduced by 36 percent, builds in massive protectionism. Minimum access is not guaranteed: only the opportunity to fill the tariff rate quotas (TRQ) is ensured, with the effectiveness depending on the margin of preference for the TRQ. Given the influence of parastatal institutions in import decisions, one can imagine circumstances in which the minimum access is never realized even if tariff rates suggest profitable imports. The pressure to find ways to preserve market share would intensify, and the carefully crafted definition of export subsidies would be put to the test. In particular, countries might experiment with two-price schemes that avoid explicit export subsidies but favor exports by allowing a lucrative domestic market to cover fixed costs. Endless questioning of the "green-box" procedures could weaken what little liberalization comes from that innovation.

Perhaps the best perspective on the Uruguay Round Agreement for Agriculture is therefore that it offers the tools for countries to improve the trade system if they wish. They can continue to pursue a course of domestic and regional reform of agricultural policies in conjunction with other economic policies. In that case the tools are at hand for the improvement of the multilateral system. The trade rules will help to contain domestic protectionism and give good external arguments for further domestic change. The trade rules also help to make regional trade agreements easier to negotiate and help to ensure that agricultural trade is fully included in those agreements.[12] The new GATT/WTO rules will not, however, be enough to drive countries in directions that they do not want to go. If policies begin to shift back to market management, one would have to conclude that even the relatively tight language of the Uruguay Round Agreement will not save the day.

---

12. For an exploration of the connection between regional trade pacts, multilateral trade rules, and agricultural policy choice, see Josling (1993).

Comment by Dale Hathaway

Dr. Josling is to be commended on his comprehensive review and balanced assessment of the results of the Uruguay Round for agreement on agriculture. My difference with his analysis rests largely on an interpretation of the results. First, I agree that the Agreement makes important changes in the trade rules for agriculture, which in the long run may revolutionize agricultural protection and trade policies. In the near and intermediate term, however, trade liberalization was sacrificed for reform of the trade rules. The Uruguay Round will provide few opportunities for low-cost producers to sell more of their products in protected markets and will do little to reduce subsidized output in countries with significant domestic subsidy programs.

The tariffication of quantitative import limitations resulted in extraordinarily high tariffs, in many cases in excess of 100 percent. Imports in excess of the quantities provided as minimum access levels are highly unlikely. In the unlikely event that trade does flow over these high tariffs, the Agreement provides for a special safeguard that can be triggered by either low import prices or a surge in imports. Apart from some notable and highly publicized exceptions, such as rice in Japan and Korea, the aggregated minimum access commitments do very little to provide access beyond current levels of imports. The binding of tariffs often occurred at levels well above the current applied tariff levels and would allow substantial increases in effective protection if the countries concerned so choose. This seems to represent modest liberalization at best.

The new rules governing export subsidies represent a considerable improvement in precision over the old rules. But they authorize the continuation of these trade-distorting practices on product quantities only 21 percent below the amounts that produced the market distortions of the late 1980s. Thus the separate treatment for agriculture that existed in the GATT was perpetuated. Moreover, the new rules limit these competitive policies to those countries rich enough or aggressive enough to use them during the base period of 1986–90. In the United States the new maximum allowable export subsidies are viewed as minimums, and export subsidies will become a regular policy tool in international competition rather than a defensive tool in combatting unfair trade practices. Assuming other countries take the same approach, it may be too optimistic to assert that the new agreement will end conflicts and market disruption.

There is another area of export competition and import controls that was untouched by the negotiations. No curbs were placed on the activities of state-trading entities, and they were not required to provide additional transparency regarding their practices. Thus the Canadian Wheat Board can continue to use discriminatory pricing as a competitive tool, and the Japanese Food Agency can purchase wheat and rice at world prices and resell them at vastly higher interior prices, using the profits to subsidize Japanese producers. It is hard to square the actions of many of these state trading entities with trade liberalization. With China poised to enter the new World Trade Organization (WTO) and still using state trading for the overwhelming proportion of its agricultural trade, the failure to deal with this issue may come back to haunt the negotiators. In any event, the actions of these entities are likely to spawn a series of trade disputes in the future, as they already have between the United States and Canada.

The Agreement will not force major domestic policy reforms or reductions in the subsidy level for individual commodities. Therefore, it is unlikely to bring improvements in world market conditions. Indeed, estimates by advocates of the agreement can find little market improvement in the agricultural agreement as such. For instance, both the United States Department of Agriculture econometric model and the FAPRI (Food and Agricultural Policy Research Institute) model of Iowa State University show trade gains and price increases as modest and due almost entirely to assumed consumer income growth from the total agreement.

The "peace clause" will not by itself guarantee peace in trade relations. It is aimed at past GATT cases; and, given the country of origin of the peace clause, an analogy to the Maginot Line does not seem inappropriate. Trade agreements do not mean an end to trade disputes; witness the current difficulties between the United States and Canada over agricultural trade. Trade disputes depend on market conditions and producer dissatisfaction in one or more of the countries involved. The same GATT rules that brought bitter conflict in the 1980s provided relative peace and quiet in the 1970s. Market conditions changed rather than the rules.

If there are trade conflicts, they are likely to occur over implementation of the agreement, especially the SPS Agreement. The United States is already charging that the EU is not implementing the oilseed agreement faithfully. Thus EU oilseed policy could easily be the first dispute, although hardly a new one, under the new agreement. It would be surprising if the old dispute over the use of growth hormones in beef production and the new one over the use of BST in milk production do not soon follow.

In the final analysis, I agree with Dr. Josling that the new agreement provides a framework for a future reduction in trade distorting policies and trade liberalization in agriculture, if countries want to move in that direction. This is likely to depend on convincing producers in countries where protection levels are still high that their well-being is not threatened by further reductions in levels of protection and further trade liberalization. It also will require political leaders who refuse to be held hostage by agricultural interests intent on perpetuating trade-distorting policies. It is indeed optimistic to assume that this unique combination of events will occur, allowing the fruits of the Uruguay Round finally to be harvested.

Discussion

Most of the general discussion focused on whether the agricultural portion of the Agreement represented any net liberalization of trade. The participants generally agreed that the benefits of the Agreement were largely in the area of establishing an improved set of rules, rather than in effecting any significant immediate trade liberalization. Julius Katz noted that it was hard to work in the area of agricultural trade policy without becoming a complete cynic, but he believed that some significant progress had been made. While the level of protection in not reduced in the near term, the new rules do place a cap on future protection, require some reduction of tariffs in future years, and provide a strong base for further negotiations in the fifth year of the agreement. Barry Bosworth noted that, while the conversion of quotas to tariffs was a noteworthy rule change, very small increases in imports trigger a special provision allowing for additional duties. In that sense the Agreement has many elements of a variable import levy. Tim Josling agreed that little liberalization had occurred on the import side, but the restrictions on export subsidies could have some immediate effect.

Dale Hathaway pointed out that the original provision for minimum access, defined as import opportunities for a 3–5 percent share of domestic consumption, would have implied liberalization, but its benefits had been largely lost by allowing countries to average across tariff lines. Thus countries could continue to exclude all imports in a specific product line by averaging them with products that have large import shares. The provision was likely to be important only for rice imports into Japan and Korea.

Michael Ferrantino raised a question about the effect of the health and safety provisions. Countries can continue to invoke their own health and safety standards, but with the proviso that they are based on sound scientific evidence. He wondered how countries would agree on what constitutes sound scientific evidence. The United States and the European Community had had several earlier disputes that centered on interpretations of scientific risk assessment studies. Dale Hathaway argued that there was some basis for defining the scientific standards by the reference in the Agreement to international organizations. He also observed that the new rules improve transparency by requiring countries to make their regulations public, a new condition.

Catherine Mann noted that the agricultural negotiations raise an issue that will recur in other areas such as environmental protection and labor standards. In agriculture many people do not begin with the presumption that freer trade is better because of the long-run efficiency gains. Instead, they argue that protection of their domestic agricultural system is an exception, involving cultural values, and they do not wish to expose it to greater competition. Thus this negotiation focused on how a country must protect its agricultural industry, if it wants to do so, in a way in which the costs are borne by the citizens of that country rather than by foreigners. Thus domestic farmers can be subsidized, but not through a system that distorts trade or otherwise pushes the costs onto foreigners. This same question of who will bear the costs arises with environmental and labor standards. Josling responded that it will be hard to distinguish among subsidies that are or are not trade-distorting. It could be argued, for example, that crop insurance, by insuring farmers against potential losses, enhances production. Thus it will be necessary to see how the agreement is implemented before judging its applicability to other areas.

References

GATT Goods Negotiating Group. 1993. Modalities for the Establishment of Specific Binding Commitments under the Reform Program. MTN.GNG/MA/W/24, Geneva, December 20.

GATT Trade Negotiations Committee. 1993. Final Act Embodying the Results of the Uruguay Round of Multilateral Trade Negotiations. MTN/FA. Geneva, December 15.

Josling, Tim. 1993. "Agriculture in a World of Trading Blocs." *Australian Journal of Agricultural Economics* (December).

Josling, Tim, and Stefan Tangermann. 1994. "The Significance of Tariffication in the Uruguay Round Agreement on Agriculture." Paper presented to the North American Agricultural Policy Research Consortium Symposium on Canadian Agricultural Policy, Vancouver, May.

Josling, Tim, and others. 1994. *The Uruguay Round Agreement on Agriculture: An Evaluation of the Outcome of the Negotiations.* International Agricultural Trade Research Consortium, Commissioned Paper No. 9. (Coauthors Masayoshi Honma, Jaewok Lee, Donald MacLaren, Bill Miner, Dan Sumner, Stefan Tangermann and Alberto Valdes.)

Tangermann, Stefan. 1994. "An Assessment of the Uruguay Round Agreement on Agriculture." Paper prepared for the Directorate for Food, Agriculture and Fisheries and the Trade Directorate of OECD, Stanford.

The World Trade Organization, Dispute Settlement, and Codes of Conduct

John H. Jackson

The Uruguay Round, the eighth broad trade negotiation round under the auspices of the General Agreement on Tariffs and Trade (GATT), is clearly the most extensive undertaken by the GATT system and possibly by any similar endeavor in history. The goals of the September 1986 ministerial meeting at Punta del Este, which set forth the agenda for the Uruguay Round, were extremely ambitious. If only half of the objectives had been achieved, the Uruguay Round would still be the most extensive and successful trade negotiation ever. In fact, despite the many years of delay and negotiating impasses, the Uruguay Round has achieved considerably more than half its objectives. Indeed, I think it is fair to say that the Uruguay Round, if satisfactorily implemented, includes nine major accomplishments, as well as a number of lesser achievements. The major accomplishments are:

—establishing a new international discipline for trade in services, comparable to that of GATT for products;

This paper is adapted largely from testimony by the author before the U.S. Senate Foreign Relations Committee, June 14, 1994, and the U.S. Senate Committee on Finance, March 23, 1994. The information on the Uruguay Round result is contained in the GATT document entitled "Final Act Embodying the Results of the Uruguay Round of Multilateral Trade Negotiations," dated March 30, 1994, but prepared for the Marrakesh, Morocco, ministerial meeting to conclude the round for April 15, 1994. Some further works by this author concerning this general subject are listed at the end of this paper.

—establishing a new international discipline for the protection of intellectual property;

—for the first time bringing trade in agricultural products under the discipline of the GATT rules;

—phasing out the anomalous international structure for trade in textiles and bringing trade in those products under the regular GATT discipline;

—integrating developing countries more fully into the GATT/WTO system, requiring schedules and eliminating certain exceptions;

—establishing some major results in the area of market access, with substantial overall tariff reductions and, in some sectors, a "zero-for-zero" result;

—establishing a new code for the troublesome subject of subsidies in international trade;

—providing a new and revised set of procedures for dispute resolution;

—launching a new institutional structure intended to facilitate and enhance implementation of the Uruguay Round results.

Of course the Uruguay Round will not be an unmixed blessing for every individual or business enterprise. That is always the case for trade negotiations, including one like this, which on balance is a strong positive for the economy. In some cases individuals with relatively little capacity, either financially or otherwise, to respond to some of the requirements of adjustment imposed by the trade agreements will need assistance from our government.

The World Trade Organization (WTO)

One of the interesting achievements of the Uruguay Round is the development of a new institutional charter for an organization that will help facilitate international cooperation concerning trade and economic relations. Some believe that this may be the most important result of the Uruguay Round. Clearly the WTO is an essential part of the total package that is required of all nations that decide to accept the Uruguay Round; it is essential for the effective implementation of the Uruguay Round results.

Genesis of the WTO

The GATT was never intended to be an organization. It was negotiated in 1947–48, while negotiators simultaneously prepared a charter for the International Trade Organization (ITO). The GATT was to be a multilateral trade and tariff agreement, which would depend for its organizational context and secretariat services on the ITO. The ITO never came into being because the U.S. Congress would not approve it in the late 1940s. The GATT, however, was negotiated under advance authority granted to the president in the 1945 extension of the Reciprocal Trade Agreements Act (the first such act was 1934). Because the ITO was still-born, the GATT gradually became the focus for international government cooperation on trade matters.

Nevertheless, despite this inauspicious beginning, the GATT has been remarkably successful over its nearly five decades of history. In part this is because of the GATT's ingenious and pragmatic leadership, particularly in its early years, when it struggled to fill the gap left by the ITO failure.

The success was particularly important in reducing tariffs, so in later years tariffs became less important than a plethora of nontariff barriers. Some of these were addressed (for the first time) in the seventh round of trade negotiations, known as the Tokyo Round (1973–79). As decades passed, however, the GATT system was recognized as being increasingly challenged by the changing conditions of international economic activity, including the greater interdependence of national economies and the growth in trade of services. Concern developed that the GATT was too handicapped to play the needed role of complementing the Bretton Woods system as the "third leg," alongside the International Monetary Fund (IMF) and the World Bank. Problems and "birth defects" included:

—provisional application and grandfather rights exceptions;
—ambiguity about the powers of the contracting parties to make certain decisions;
—ambiguity regarding the waiver authority and risks of misuse;
—murky legal status leading to misunderstanding by the public, the media, and even government officials;
—certain defects in the dispute settlement procedures;
—general lack of institutional provisions, requiring constant improvisation.

In December 1991, the Uruguay Round negotiators led by the GATT director general, Arthur Dunkel, prepared and released a draft text of treaty clauses covering the entire Uruguay Round negotiation results up to that point, with indications of work yet to do. This was an important project with many implications. Included in this draft was, for the first time, a tentative draft of a new charter for an organization—the Multilateral Trade Organization (MTO). This draft had a number of flaws, recognized by the U.S. government and others, but through hard work the negotiators were able to revise the draft and iron out the flaws. In the December 1993 draft the new organization was retitled the World Trade Organization (WTO), and it is this draft charter that I will discuss.

What Is the WTO?

Let me begin by suggesting four general characteristics and advantages of the WTO Charter in the Uruguay Round draft texts.

First, the WTO can be described as a mini-charter. It is devoted to the institutional and procedural structure that will facilitate and in some cases be necessary for effective implementation of the substantive rules that have been negotiated in the Uruguay Round. The WTO is not an ITO (the 1948 ITO draft charter, which never came into force). The WTO Charter itself is entirely institutional and procedural, but it incorporates the substantive agreements resulting from the Uruguay Round into annexes. In many cases the criticism aimed at the WTO is really criticism aimed at some of the substantive provisions of the Uruguay Round results and should not be considered a criticism of the WTO institutional charter.

Second, the WTO essentially will continue the GATT institutional ideas and many of its practices, in a form better understood by the public, media, government officials, and lawyers. To some small extent, a number of the GATT birth defects are overcome in the WTO. The WTO Charter (article XVI:I) states the intention to be guided by GATT "decisions, procedures and customary practices" to the extent feasible. The practice of consensus is better defined and for the first time becomes a legal procedure in some important decisions rather than just a practice.

Third, the WTO structure offers some important advantages for assisting the effective implementation of the Uruguay Round. For example, a "new GATT 1994" is created to supersede the "old GATT." This procedure avoids the constraints of the amending clause of the old GATT, which might make it quite difficult to bring the Uruguay Round into legal force. At the same time, the WTO ties together the various texts developed in the Uruguay Round and reinforces the "single package" idea of the negotiators—namely, that countries accepting the Uruguay Round must accept the entire package (with a few exceptions). No longer will the Tokyo Round approach of side codes, resulting in "GATT à la carte," be the norm.

The WTO Charter establishes (for the first time) the basic explicit legal authority for a secretariat, a director-general, and staff. It does this in a way similar to many other international organizations, and it also adds the obligation for nations to avoid interfering with the officials of the organization.

Another important aspect of the WTO structure is that it facilitates the extension of the institutional structure (GATT-like) to the new subjects negotiated in the Uruguay Round, particularly services and intellectual property. Without some kind of legal mechanism such as the WTO, this would have been quite difficult to do, since the GATT itself applies only to goods. The new GATT structure separates the institutional concepts from the substantive rules. The GATT 1994 will remain a substantive agreement (with many of the amendments and improvements developed throughout its history, including in the Uruguay Round). The WTO has a broader context.

Similarly, the WTO will be able to apply a unified mechanism for settling disputes and the Trade Policy Review Mechanism. These will extend to all of the subjects covered by the Uruguay Round for all nations that become members.

Fourth, the WTO Charter offers considerably better opportunities for the future evolution and development of the institutional structure for international trade cooperation. Even though the WTO Charter is minimalist, the fact that it provides for explicit legal status and the traditional organizational structure helps in this regard. With the WTO focusing on the institutional side, it also offers more flexibility for future inclusion of new negotiated rules or measures that can assist nations to face the constantly emerging problems of world economics.

In the United States and some other countries, the question has been raised whether the WTO is too intrusive on "national sovereignty." A careful examination of the WTO Charter leads me to conclude that the WTO has no more real power than that which existed for the GATT under the previous agreements. This may seem surprising, but in fact the GATT treaty text contained language that was quite ambiguous and could have been misused (but fortunately was not) to provide rather extensive powers. For example, in article XXV of the GATT the contracting parties acting by majority vote were given the authority to take joint action "with a view to facilitating the operation and furthering the objectives of this agreement." This is very broad and ambiguous language. The WTO Charter gives considerably more attention to the question of decisionmaking in a number of different contexts, and certain restraints have been added: increasing the voting requirements for certain actions (to three-fourths of the members for many waivers and for formal interpretations); providing in the amending clauses that a country will not be bound by an amendment that it opposes if the amendment would "alter the rights and obligations of the members." Likewise, the waiver authority is more constrained and will be harder to abuse. Furthermore, formal "interpretations" "shall not be used in the manner that would undermine the amendment provisions." Thus there are more legal grounds to challenge overreaching of the power of the WTO institutions.

Regarding the practice of "consensus" as established for several decades in the GATT, several characteristics are worth noting. The GATT makes no explicit indication of a "consensus practice"; indeed, the word "consensus" is not used. The consensus practice developed partly as a result of the uneasiness of governments about the loose wording of GATT decisionmaking powers, particularly that in GATT article XXV. Partly because of this uneasiness, the practice developed of avoiding strict voting. Instead, the contracting parties have for several decades made virtually all of their decisions by "consensus." Even when a formal vote was required (such as for a waiver), there would generally be a negotiation for a consensus draft text before such text was submitted to capitals for the formal vote.

In the practice of GATT, however, the word "consensus" was not defined. In the legal sense, if some sort of "consensus" could not be achieved, the fallback was the loose voting authority of the GATT. In the WTO Charter, however, consensus is defined (at least for some purposes) as the situation when a decision occurs and "no member, present at the meeting when the decision is taken, formally objects to the proposed decision." It should be noted that this is not the same as unanimity, since consensus is defeated only by a formal objection by a member present at the meeting. Thus those absent do not prevent a consensus, nor does an abstention prevent a consensus. Furthermore, the practice in GATT and surely also in WTO is that some countries that have difficulty with a particular decision will nevertheless remain silent out of deference to countries with a substantially higher stake in the pragmatic economic consequences of a decision. Thus the consensus practice itself involves some deference to economic power. This has certainly been the practice in the GATT, and the WTO Charter provides that the WTO shall be guided by such "customary practices."

The WTO is considerably more explicit about the situation in which consensus fails. In a few instances, a decision must be by consensus and there is no fallback to a majority vote. (For example, adding plurilateral agreements to annex 4, article X:9 and amendments to the dispute settlement procedures in annex 2.) In many other situations, when consensus fails there is an explicit fallback vote, such as three-fourths of the membership. It is considered quite difficult to achieve such a heavy fallback vote as three-fourths of the membership (not three-fourths of those voting), since often 25 percent of the membership is not involved in a particular decision and may not show up at the meeting.

Thus the protection of national sovereignty built into the WTO Charter rules on decisionmaking are substantially enhanced over that of the GATT.

The amending authority (article X) is itself quite intricate and ingenious. It obviously has been carefully tailored to the needs of the participating nations related to each of the different major multilateral agreements (GATT, GATS [Services], and intellectual property). Amendments for some parts of these require unanimity. Other parts require two-thirds (after procedures in the Ministerial Conference and Councils seeking consensus for amendment proposals). In most all cases, as mentioned above, when an amendment would "alter the rights and obligations," a member that refuses to accept the amendment is not bound by it. In such a case, however, there is an ingenious procedure (partly following the model in the GATT) whereby the Ministerial Conference can by three-fourths vote of the members require all to accept the amendment, withdraw from the agreement, or remain a member with explicit consent of the Ministerial Conference. Quite frankly, it is therefore very hard to conceive of the amending provisions being used in any way to force a major trading country such as the United States to accept altered rights or obligations. As stated above, the spirit and practice of the GATT has always been to try to accommodate through consensus negotiation procedures the views of as many countries as possible, but certainly to give weight to views of countries that have great weight in the trading system. This will not change.

Dispute Settlement Procedures

One of the many achievements of the GATT, despite its "birth defects," has been the development of a reasonably sophisticated process for settling disputes. The original GATT treaty contained very little on this, although it did specifically provide (in articles XXII and XXIII) for consultation, and then submittal of issues to the GATT contracting parties. As time went on, however, the practice began to evolve more toward a "rule oriented" system. For example, in the late 1950s the practice introduced a "panel" of individuals to make determinations and findings and recommend them to the contracting parties. Before that, disputes had been considered in much broader working parties comprising representatives of governments.

In the Uruguay Round 1994 text, there is a major new area concerning dispute settlement procedures, the "Understanding on Rules and Procedures Governing the Settlement of Disputes." The new text solves many of the issues that have plagued the GATT dispute settlement system, although not all of them.

—It establishes a unified dispute settlement system for all parts of the GATT/WTO system, including the new subjects of services and intellectual property. Thus controversies over which procedure to use will not occur.
—It reaffirms the right of a complaining government to have a panel process initiated, preventing blocking at that stage.
—It ingeniously establishes a new appellate procedure that will substitute for some of the council approval process of a panel report and overcome blocking. Thus a panel report will automatically be deemed adopted by the council unless it is appealed by one of the parties to the dispute. If appealed, the dispute will go to an appellate panel. After the appellate body has ruled, its report will go to the council, but in this case it will be deemed adopted unless there is a consensus *against* adoption, and presumably that negative consensus can be defeated by any major objector. Thus the presumption is reversed, compared with the previous procedures, and the result of the procedure is that the appellate report will in virtually every case come into force as a matter of international law.

It should, however, be understood that the international legal system does not embrace the common law jurisprudence that prevails in the United States, which calls for courts to operate under a stricter "precedent" or stare decisis rule. Most nations in the world do not have stare decisis as part of their legal systems, and the international law also does not. This means that technically a GATT panel report is not strict precedent, although there is certainly some tendency for subsequent GATT panels to follow what they deem to be the "wisdom" of earlier panel reports. Nevertheless, a GATT panel has the option not to follow a previous panel report, and this has occurred in several cases. In addition, although an adopted panel report will generally provide an international law obligation for the participants in the dispute to follow the report, the GATT contracting parties acting in a council or the ministerial conference can make interpretive rulings or resolutions that would depart from that GATT panel ruling; they can even establish a waiver to relieve a particular obligation. It is clear both that no system will be perfect and that not all cases will be decided in the most appropriate way. There will be mistakes. There will be situations where the United States or other countries will lose cases that they should lose; but also there will be cases in which the United States and others will lose cases they did not deserve to lose. This is not different from domestic legal processes. Nevertheless, in the broader context there is a great deal of utility in a creditable and efficient, rule-oriented dispute settlement system that has integrity, and the United States is an important beneficiary of such a system.

It is quite interesting how significant dispute settlement systems have become in major international trade agreements in the last decades. For example, such a system is a very intricate part of the European Union with its Court of Justice sitting in Luxembourg. It is also an important and enhanced part of the U.S.-Canada Free Trade Agreement, the North American Free Trade Agreement (NAFTA), and other similar regional arrangements that are currently evolving.

"Rules" in the Final Act

As indicated above, there is a major difference in the approach of the Uruguay Round results compared with the Tokyo Round of the 1970s. This is particularly apparent concerning various sets of "rules" of trade behavior that are set forth in the results of these two rounds. In the Tokyo Round, the results included nine separate agreements concerning trade conduct "rules" as follows:

—technical barriers to trade
—government procurement
—interpretation and application of articles VI, XVI, and XXIII (subsidies)
—arrangement regarding bovine meat
—international dairy arrangement
—implementation of article VII (custom valuation)
—import licensing procedures
—trade in civil aircraft
—implementation of article VI (antidumping duties)

None of these agreements strictly "amended" the GATT even though some of them carried a title suggesting "interpretation" of some GATT clauses. Each of these agreements was technically a stand-alone "treaty," sometimes called a "code of conduct." Each GATT contracting party (nation) could decide which of these agreements to accept (GATT à la carte). This result has been strongly criticized, and indeed even the most accepted of these 1979 agreements had less than half the GATT "membership" as parties.

In the Uruguay Round the negotiators determined from an early date not to repeat this feature of the Tokyo Round, but to strive instead for a "single package" approach that required all nations that accepted the Uruguay Round results to accept the entire package. With a few exceptions this is the structure of the result of the Uruguay Round.

The WTO sets up the overall framework for implementing the Uruguay Round with the WTO Charter as the "umbrella agreement" dealing only with institutional matters, but the substantive results contained in annexes to the WTO charter. There are four annexes.

Annex 1 contains the "multilateral agreements," which include the three major parts of the substantive results of the Uruguay Round, namely:

1A = GATT 1994 (to be distinguished from GATT 1947, the old GATT);
1B = GATS or General Agreement on Trade in Services;
1C = TRIPS or agreement on Trade-Related Intellectual Property matters.

These agreements are part of the mandatory provisions of the "single package," required for all members of the WTO, along with annexes 2 and 3.

Annex 2 contains the dispute settlement procedures (as described above); annex 3 contains the TPRM, which is the Trade Policy Review Mechanism; annex 4 contains the "plurilateral agreements," which are not mandatory and those are a modest concession to some choice for members. At the moment these agreements are:

Agreement on Trade in Civil Aircraft
Agreement on Government Procurement
International Dairy Agreement
International Bovine Meat Agreement

The last two of these "agreements" are rather ambiguous statements without much real obligation. The first two seem more directed to industrial countries and thus were chosen for this optional status. As noted earlier, the concept of annex 4 opens up the possibility for easier addition of new subjects, on a sort of trial basis, as the WTO evolves and tries to cope with fast-changing economic realities.

Annex 1A contains the GATT 1994, which is essentially the old GATT as it has been modified by amendments and many of the Tokyo Round "codes" as updated in the Uruguay Round, as well as some new agreements resulting in the Uruguay Round. Thus appended to the GATT 1994 are such agreements as:

Agreement on Agriculture
Agreement on Sanitary and Phytosanitary Measures
Agreement on Textiles and Clothing
Agreement on Technical Barriers to Trade
Agreement on Trade-Related Investment Measures
Agreement on Antidumping
Agreement on Valuation
Agreement on Preshipment Inspection
Agreement on Rules of Origin
Agreement on Import Licensing
Agreement on Subsidies and Countervailing Measures
Agreement on Safeguards

plus a series of "understandings," which further modify the GATT, and some ministerial "decisions and declarations."

Two of these agreements, now part of the GATT 1994, concern what are probably the most contentious of the "rules of conduct" clauses of the GATT, namely Antidumping and Subsidies/Countervailing. One other concerns product standards (technical barriers) also addressed in the Sanitary and Phytosanitary Agreement. The Agreement on Safeguards could also be a very important result of the Uruguay Round, addressing a subject on which the Tokyo Round failed to achieve agreement. The relationship of these various GATT additions to the core GATT agreement itself is not always clear.

The GATT 1994 (to say nothing of the GATS and TRIPS agreements) now addresses a very large array of "rules" and thus comprises an ambitious "code of conduct" addressing important issues. It is not possible in this paper, however, to elaborate on the details of these rules except perhaps to say that there is a general perception that the antidumping rules have not been very much improved by the Uruguay Round, while the Subsidies/Countervailing provisions have been greatly improved conceptually, though several "exception" provisions are ambiguous enough to have the potential to cause difficulty.

U.S. Law and the WTO

There is some confusion about the effect of a WTO and its actions on U.S. law. It is almost certain to be the case (as Congress has provided in recent trade agreements) that the WTO and the Uruguay Round agreements will not be self-executing in U.S. law. Thus they do not automatically become part of U.S. law. Nor do the results of panel dispute settlement procedures automatically become part of U.S. law. Instead the United States must implement the international obligations or the result of a panel report, often through legislation adopted by the Congress. In a case where the United States feels it is so important to deviate from the international norms that it is willing to do so knowing that it may be acting inconsistently with its international obligations, the U.S. government still has that power under its constitutional system. This can be an important constraint if matters go seriously wrong. This power should not be lightly used, of course. In addition, it should be noted again that governments as members of the WTO have the right to withdraw from the WTO with a mere six months notice (article XV:I). This is a drastic action, unlikely to be taken, but it does provide some checks and balances to the overall system.

Clearly, the United States is so important to the success of the WTO and the trading rules that, as a practical matter, the United States cannot be ignored. Indeed, some of the more specific rules of the WTO will reinforce deference to this position.

The question has been raised whether the new GATT/WTO dispute settlement procedures of the Uruguay Round results will require fundamental changes in the Section 301 statutes of the United States. Most people recall that Section 301 provides a procedure for individual enterprises in the United States initiating U.S. government attention to alleged foreign government practices that harm U.S. commerce, mostly targeted on U.S. exports, but also applicable to matters such as intellectual property, subsidized imports, and service trade.

It appears that very few statutory changes will be needed to U.S. Section 301, at least the "regular 301" (compared with Special 301 and other similar statutory provisions, such as those on telecommunications.) There may need to be some alterations to some time limits, or transition measures, but the basic structure of 301 is not necessarily inconsistent with the Uruguay Round results. Section 301 when appropriately used in its current statutory form can be a constructive measure for U.S. trade policy and for world trade policy. Section 301 calls for cases presented under the 301 procedural framework to be taken to the international dispute settlement process that pertains to the case. Likewise, Section 301 in its present formulation does not *require* the executive branch to ignore the results of the international dispute settlement process. Thus the executive appears to have the discretion to apply actions under

Section 301 in a manner consistent with the proposed new rules of the Uruguay Round dispute settlement understanding.

Although there are plausible ways to interpret the statutory provisions of regular Section 301 so as to give the president discretion to act consistently with the Uruguay Round dispute settlement rules, in a few cases, particularly in Section 301(a) (the mandatory provision), the interpretations to do this are a bit strained. It would clearly therefore be better if the statute were amended to give the president and the trade representative in all cases under the statute the discretion to act in a way consistent with U.S. international obligations. Alternatively the Statement of Administrative Action by the President, along with other legislative history, could clarify this position.

However, to be candid one must realize that the procedures of the new dispute settlement understanding will provide moderately more pressure on all governments that will be members of the WTO to conform to the results of a dispute settlement process. Partly this is because the new dispute settlement procedures include a segment dealing explicitly with the question of responses available to a complaining state, when a defending member of WTO does not conform to its obligations after a dispute settlement procedure. Of course a nation can still refuse to conform. For example, this could mean that despite a ruling against the United States on a complaint brought by the United States, the president might be tempted to take action that he is authorized to take under Section 301. Such action could be the violation of international obligations. The mere existence of the possible hypothetical authority to take such action would not necessarily be a violation.

In several instances in the 1980s the United States took unilateral and independent action without proceeding through the GATT. These would be inconsistent with the new rules. However, they were also inconsistent with the old rules, to the extent that actual trade restraining measures were applied at the border that violated the GATT (such as an increase in tariffs).

Comment by Julius L. Katz

John Jackson has provided an excellent overview of the institutional aspects of the Uruguay Round: the WTO, dispute settlement, and the various agreements that are a part of the overall package.

I particularly liked the balance of the paper. I agree with Jackson's description of the benefits of the WTO, yet he describes it as a modest charter and, indeed, it is. The WTO is a bare-bones institution. In fact, in many ways, as he has pointed out, it is an institutionalization of the existing GATT and the practices that have developed with respect to the GATT over the years. It makes de jure what has become de facto.

But the WTO goes beyond that in providing an umbrella for a series of agreements: the new GATT (GATT, 1994), as well as agreements on services (the GATS), the TRIPS agreement, and intellectual property, and the other associated compacts. I believe that this is one of the major benefits, bringing all these agreements together in a single institution. The "single undertaking," which requires WTO members to accept all obligations, will greatly reduce the à la carte game in which countries accept those obligations they like and not the others. Another major advance is in the voting procedures, which Jackson has described in detail.

Just by way of historical perspective, we did not, initially, embrace the idea of a WTO. There were a number of reasons for that. When the Canadians presented the idea of a Multilateral Trade Organization, in the summer or autumn of 1990, we were within several months of what was to have been the conclusion of the Round. I recall saying at the time: This was an idea that had come both too late and too early. It was too late for the Uruguay Round and too early for the next round of negotiations. As it turned out, of course, we did not conclude at the end of 1990, and the negotiations went on.

The idea was then embraced by the European Community, in part for defensive reasons. It was in a highly defensive position with respect to agriculture, which was the issue that prevented the conclusion of the negotiations at the end of 1990. The Community put a twist on the Canadian proposal and used it as a way to attack what it referred to as U.S. unilateralism.

The final reason we were not enamored of the proposal is that we had other priorities in the negotiations, and we viewed the WTO as a distraction.

What happened next was that the Community produced a draft. The Canadian proposal was just barely an outline of an idea. The Community's legal text was very flawed, but it was adopted by the director general of the GATT, Arthur Dunkel, who included the EC text in his draft final act. We had serious problems with that text. There were a number of ambiguities and provisions that we just flat out disagreed with.

I said earlier in the discussion of agriculture that something was lost in the last twelve months of the negotiations. With respect to the WTO, however, there was a considerable improvement. In fact, we had largely given up on the WTO as provided for in the Dunkel text, and, partly for tactical reasons, we submitted an alternative proposal that was to incorporate all the advantages of the WTO without the WTO itself. We proposed a declaration that would have provided for the single undertaking, the common dispute settlement mechanism, and some of the benefits, but without the trappings of the institution itself.

For a long time there has been a paradoxical view of a multilateral trading organization in the United States. On the one hand, the GATT has been criticized for being ineffective. It is jokingly referred to as the General Agreement to Talk and Talk. It does not do anything. Decisionmaking is too difficult and takes too long. Dispute settlement is ineffective.

On the other hand, there is a sensitivity about anything that suggests a loss of sovereignty. That was, in large part, the issue that sank the ITO, and it has reared its head again recently in the debate over the WTO. As Jackson has pointed out, there is, really, very little to the sovereignty argument with respect to the WTO.

Because of the voting system and some other aspects, this is not an organization in the same sense as the other economic organizations: the International Monetary Fund or the World Bank. Nor is it a World Court with respect to dispute settlements.

Thus there is some good news and some bad news here. On the one hand, we cannot be outvoted. None of what happens in the GATT or the WTO automatically becomes U.S. law. The Congress has to enact any changes in obligations. But, on the other hand, this new institution will still lack effectiveness of the kind that sometimes we seek.

Much will depend on how the institution is managed. And, that, of course, critically, depends, first of all, on the leadership at the top. Unfortunately, the current director general, Peter Sutherland, has announced that he will not continue in office after the end of this year, so there will be a search for a new director general. I think Jackson is right in saying that the WTO has raised the profile of the institution so that people have set their sights higher in terms of the kind of person who will fill that job; even a head of government is in the running.

But beyond that, the institution needs to evolve in a way that leads to a better management structure. The council is unwieldy. There are now 120 countries. Theoretically, every country in the WTO can sit in the council. As a matter of practice, only about fifty or sixty turn up at any one time. But even that is highly unwieldy. What is required is a small regular group of not more than twenty countries that can help in giving the institution policy direction.

Finally, a great deal will depend on what the United States puts into this. The United States is the largest and one of the most dominant players. Nothing has happened in the past without U.S. leadership, and nothing will in the future. So we are bound to have a major role in shaping the future of this institution.

Comment by Clyde Prestowitz

I think my role here is to be something of a critic. Therefore, I want to preface my remarks by saying that I think many of the benefits that Jackson and Katz described are valid. There are going to be significant gains for the United States as a result of a number of the Uruguay Round provisions that will be encompassed in the WTO.

But in the spirit of being provocative, let me point to some of the areas where I think there are valid concerns and places where there are potential weaknesses or the potential for negative effect on U.S. interests exists.

First, I think that, inevitably, there will be a loss of sovereignty. You can argue whether that is good or bad. I think it is reasonable to say that in a world of integrating economies there needs to be some institution under which that integration takes place and, inevitably, that carries with it some degree of loss of sovereignty.

So, I am not sure that the loss of sovereignty itself is, necessarily, a decisive issue; but I do think that the environmentalists, in particular, are correct when they express their concern for the potential reversal of U.S. regulations via findings of the WTO.

One that you are all familiar with is the question of U.S. CAFE standards (automobile gas mileage requirements) and whether or not those and the accompanying gas-guzzler tax are de facto trade impediments and whether or not the rules of the GATT or the WTO would compel the United States to change its mileage requirements. That is one example, but there are others that can be cited, and I think they are not entirely without validity. It does not mean that there should not be a WTO, but it does mean that you should think hard about how to handle those kinds of issues when they arise.

Second, I think that the dispute settlement panels, combined with, effectively, mandatory acceptance of dispute panel decisions carry some potential for negative effect on the United States in the following sense.

The United States is an outlier among trading nations in the sense that our attitudes regarding the proper relationships between industry and government, transparency, due process, and so forth tend to be at odds with those of most of our major trading partners.

Since the members of dispute panels will inevitably be a majority non-American, the attitudes that are brought to these dispute panels are likely, in many cases, not to be compatible with our own, creating the potential for a number of decisions that would go against what we would consider to be our interests. Since we would no longer have the ability to block the panels, there could be some significant negative effect on us.

The counter argument has been made—and I think there is some validity to it—that, "Look, the United States is such a big part of the trading system and such an important member of the GATT that nobody is going to do anything that is, really, seriously going to go against U.S. interests."

That, of course, is an argument that says, "Hey, we are just so powerful that nobody can afford to antagonize us." There is, probably, some truth in that, but I think the intellectual, logical conclusion of that argument is that you should not want to be in a WTO at all because if you are so powerful, then clearly you have maximum influence in a series of bilateral negotiations with weaker opponents.

So I would not use that argument to say that we should reject the WTO, but I do think the potential is there for some negative effect on U.S. interests. It has to do with the combination of the WTO dispute settlement procedures, the lack of coverage by the WTO of some of the most important issues that give rise to trade frictions, and the application of U.S. unfair trade laws.

With the change in dispute settlement procedures making panel findings essentially mandatory, the United States obviously loses the ability to block panel findings. As others have pointed out, that will be a plus when we win the panels, but it also has potential negatives if we lose.

The real problem, it seems to me, is not so much whether you win or lose on issues that are covered by GATT rules. The biggest trade friction problems have been arising in recent years and will continue to arise over issues of competition, what the Europeans would call competition policy: cartel-like activities; noncompetitive business practices; informal arrangements between governments and companies; closed distribution systems; all of the so-called nontariff barriers that have been so much in dispute over the past ten or fifteen years. Most of these do not fall under the rules of the new WTO.

In the past, the United States has attempted to attack these issues—I would not argue that the efforts have met with any great success—through a combination of negotiation and implicit threat of application of U.S. unfair trade rules.

Of course, there has been great dispute over 301 and whether it is useful and whether it is not. Ironically, I myself testified against Super 301. Nevertheless, the potential for the application of 301 has, certainly, been a catalyst to negotiation in a number of instances.

Under the new WTO rules, I think it is reasonable to think that many trading countries are going to look at the trading situation, and they are going to say to themselves: "Well, the Americans are urging us to enter into negotiations over our nontariff barriers. Let them take us to the WTO."

So, the Americans go to the WTO, and the WTO says, "Well, really, there is no rule here, so there is, really, nothing we can do."

The U.S. side is then in the position of continuing to urge the offender to negotiate, but the offender has no real reason to negotiate because he knows that if the United States applies 301, the United States will be in violation of its WTO obligations and subject to retaliation.

The incentive for negotiation, over some of the most difficult and most important trade barriers, is, it seems to me, somewhat diminished, unless, in the implementing language of the ratification bill, that issue can be addressed.

The last point I would make is a corollary to that. If any of that reasoning is correct, it is going to mean that the most significant trade friction problems will not be resolved. The WTO will not be able to resolve them. And, as it is seen not to be resolving them, then frustration—particularly from the American side—with the whole process is going to mount, threatening the credibility of the WTO and any successive negotiations.

Discussion

The discussion focused on the system of dispute resolution. Joseph Greenwald expressed concern that the new system, which he characterized as a shift from allowing for a veto to requiring unanimity, will not work as well as continuing to seek evolutionary changes in the old system. Under the earlier system, countries could block the formation of dispute panels or publication of their findings. Under the new system, panels may rule against a country; and, if the country refuses to respond, the complaining country can retaliate. However, there are very few countries that can effectively retaliate against a large country, such as the United States. Thus the new system is likely to be very discriminatory against the smaller countries. He thought that the old system was evolving in a way that was more promising than the new system.

David Richardson also expressed concern that the new system would be discredited because the large actors would be just as slow as before to take corrective action. John Jackson agreed that this was a concern, and it was reflected in U.S. implementing legislation requiring that responses to a whole series of potential complaints would require congressional approval. The interest groups could then block any U.S. corrective action. However, any country that consistently refused to respond to the complaints of others would have trouble bringing its own. How the United States participates in the new system will be very important; but the United States is usually perceived as a principal beneficiary of a stronger dispute settlement process.

Julius Katz also pointed out that there is nothing in the new agreement that makes the situation worse than before. Claude Barfield maintained that the basic problem of getting countries to abide by the rules was not fundamentally changed by the creation of the WTO. Catherine Mann, however, noted that an effective dispute settlement was fundamental to future progress. Without it, the rules on trade were useless. She suggested that the experience with the U.S.-Canada dispute settlements indicated that such systems could make some progress, even though there were some issues of long-standing disagreement that no dispute mechanism was going to resolve.

Alan Deardorff asked why the dispute settlement process could not be made more open. John Jackson responded that there had always been two alternative approaches: the diplomatic idea of secret negotiations aimed at resolution, versus an adjudication approach. Over time, the system has moved in the direction of greater emphasis on adjudication, but the carry-over of attitudes from the diplomatic approach slows the move toward greater transparency. He saw the WTO as the beginning of a more open process, but more will have to be done in the future.

Robert Lawrence commented that Jackson's argument that the new WTO implied no greater loss of sovereignty than under the old GATT, because the prior agreement contained language that could have been interpreted as a major restriction on sovereignty, was not very appealing to those who worried about the issue. Jackson responded that any expansion of relations with other countries must involve some loss of independent action or sovereignty. In a more meaningful sense, he thought we should be certain that any international system incorporates adequate checks and balances to ensure that the system is not abused to our detriment. He thought that those checks and balances were present in the WTO, in part because initially it is little more than an organizational framework.

Clyde Prestowitz raised the issue of the extent to which the new GATT would affect U.S. regulations such as the CAFE standards that impose average mileage standards on automobiles, the gas-guzzler tax, or the restriction on imports of tuna caught by methods that kill dolphins. Katz responded that it was very likely that the United States would be found in violation of the GATT on some of these issues. That has happened in the past, and it is likely in the future. We cannot assume that actions of the U.S. Congress can simply be imposed on other countries. In such cases, some accommodation will have to be worked out. Jackson noted that the fleet average requirements of the CAFE standards do discriminate against foreign firms that sell a single model of car in the United States, compared with the large number of different cars produced by domestic producers. It might require some accommodation; but, again, no international body can dictate a specific resolution to which the United States is opposed. Instead, the United States will be pressed to find solutions that are not obviously discriminatory toward foreign firms. As in the past, it will be a negotiated compromise.

Joseph Greenwald asked what would happen to countries that signed the old GATT but opt not to join the new WTO. Would they be able to keep the benefits of the old GATT, such as MFN, without accepting the new rules? John Jackson responded that the situation was unlikely to arise. The vast majority of countries have already announced their intention to join the new GATT. Nonmembers of the new GATT could not force others to grant them MFN status with regard to the new round of tariff reductions, because the old GATT contained a provision for withdrawal with sixty days notice. The United States, for example, he thought, would probably elect to withdraw formally from the old GATT. Instead, members are likely to make various de facto provisions for countries that elect not to join, depending on their reasons. Thus in a practical sense the old GATT is dead.

Further works on the subject by John H. Jackson

————. 1967. "The General Agreement on Tariffs and Trade in United States Domestic Law." *Michigan Law Review* 66 (December): 249.

————. 1969. *World Trade and the Law of GATT* (Bobbs-Merrill).

————. 1987. "United States." In *The Effect of Treaties in Domestic Law*, edited by Francis G. Jacobs and Shelley Roberts. London: Sweet and Maxwell.

————. 1989. *The World Trading System: Law & Policy of International Economic Relations*. MIT Press.

————. 1990. *Restructuring the GATT System*. London: The Royal Institute for International Affairs.

————. 1992. "Status of Treaties in Domestic Legal Systems: A Policy Analysis." *American Journal of International Law* 86 (April): 310–40.

————. 1992. "World Trade Rules and Environmental Policies: Congruence or Conflict?" *Washington & Lee Law Review* 49 (Fall): 1227–78.

————. 1993. "Regional Trade Blocs and GATT." *World Economy* 16 (March): 121–31.

————and William J. Davey. 1986. *Legal Problems of International Economic Relations—Cases*. 2d ed. West Publishing Company.

Services and Intellectual Property Rights

Bernard Hoekman

After seven years of intensive discussions, the Uruguay Round of multilateral trade negotiations was concluded on December 15, 1993. Participating countries agreed to establish a new World Trade Organization (WTO), which, among other things, is to administer three multilateral trade agreements: the already existing General Agreement on Tariffs and Trade (GATT) as amended during the negotiations (the so-called GATT 1994), as well as the newly created General Agreement on Trade in Services (GATS) and the Agreement on Trade-Related Intellectual Property Rights (TRIPs). With the establishment of the WTO, much of the original intention of the creators of the Bretton Woods system will be realized—albeit more than forty-five years later than intended. In contrast to the GATT, which is only a treaty, the WTO will have the formal status of an international organization, on a par with the World Bank and the International Monetary Fund (IMF). Of the many agreements reached in the Uruguay Round, the GATS and the TRIPs Agreement are of particular interest because they not only extend the reach of the multilateral trading system to services and intellectual property (IP) protection (the GATT only applies to trade in goods), but also go beyond the GATT by addressing

The author is grateful to Jagdish Bhagwati, Barry Bosworth, Carlos Primo Braga, Alan Deardorff, John Jackson, Adrian Otten, and Arvind Subramanian for helpful discussions and remarks. The views expressed in this paper are personal and should not be attributed to the World Bank. Much of the analysis of the GATS draws on Hoekman and Sauvé (1994).

investment policies and domestic regulatory regimes as well as trade policies.[1] These agreements may therefore provide a foundation for future multilateral efforts to agree on rules relating to investment and market access more generally.

While a significant achievement, the GATS is only a first step. It is important to keep this in mind when assessing the agreement. Policies affecting international transactions in services were new issues for most trade negotiators, and the negotiating process was characterized by a large element of "learning by doing." It should come as no surprise that the GATS does not imply a move to free trade in services. Indeed, analogous to the GATT, that is not its objective. Under the GATT, recurring rounds of negotiations during the past five decades have helped to bring average tariffs down gradually to very low levels and discipline the use of nontariff measures. With the creation of the GATS, nations are starting down a similar path, one that is likely to take as long to traverse.

GATS is similar to the GATT in that the objective was to liberalize access to markets. The TRIPs agreement is a different kind of entity; here the objective was to agree to minimum standards of IP protection. The TRIPs agreement is more far-reaching than the GATS in the sense that it entails much more in the way of harmonization of policies and specific, generally binding obligations. This reflects the fact that TRIPs was less of a "new" issue for policymakers, although it was new for most trade negotiators. International conventions and institutions already existed on IP. The main issue on the table was to apply these and introduce TRIPs into the multilateral trading system, thereby allowing for its dispute settlement mechanism to be applicable.

Both agreements are complex and important. Relatively more attention is devoted to the GATS in what follows. In part this is because the GATS is arguably the less transparent of the two agreements. More important, the GATS is more likely be the "higher profile" agreement in the longer run, in the sense that very much remains to be done to effectively liberalize access to service markets and further develop multilateral disciplines.

---

1. A separate agreement on trade-related investment measures (TRIMs) was also negotiated. However, the TRIMs agreement is closely tied to the GATT, basically stating that GATT rules (especially national treatment and the rules against quotas) apply to TRIMs and giving GATT members a timetable to bring their policies in conformity with the GATT. Investment policies more generally are not addressed. The TRIMs agreement is comparable to those on textiles and clothing or the elimination and ban of voluntary export restraints, in that already existing GATT disciplines were reaffirmed.

Services

Until the early 1980s, trade in services was mostly ignored by policymakers and analysts. Driven by innovations in information technology, increasing specialization and product differentiation, as well as government policies such as deregulation and liberalization, trade in services grew faster than trade in merchandise throughout the past decade. As shown in table 4-1, in 1992 global services trade (defined by the GATT secretariat as nonfactor services in the balance of payments minus government transactions plus labor income) stood at some $1 trillion, or 21.1 percent of global trade (goods plus services). Such trade occurs across borders (that is, via telecommunications media), via physical movement of consumers (for example, tourism), or via temporary entry of providers (for example, consulting). The average annual growth rate of services trade over the past decade was 9.5 percent, as compared with 7.1 percent for merchandise.[2] Both industrialized and developing countries have seen the relative importance of trade in services increase, although services account for a larger share of the total trade of OECD countries. As many services are *not* tradable, producers of such services generally must contest foreign markets through foreign direct investment (FDI). Not surprisingly, FDI in services accounts for a large share of the total stock of inward FDI in most host countries. As of the early 1990s, some 50 percent of the global *stock* of FDI was in services activities. The share of annual flows to many countries has often been much higher in recent years.[3]

The Architecture of the GATS

The GATS contains two sets of obligations: (1) a set of general concepts, principles, and rules that create obligations that apply to all measures affecting trade in services; and (2) specific negotiated obligations that constitute commitments that apply to those service sectors and subsectors that are listed in a member country's schedule. The Agreement also contains a set of attachments that include annexes that take into account sectoral specificities and various

2. Services trade data are less comprehensive and reliable than those available for merchandise. Growth rates may be biased upward because of recent efforts by some OECD countries to improve collection of services trade data. The total value of trade is likely to be significantly underreported, however.

3. See UNCTAD and World Bank (1994) for data on FDI in services.

Table 4–1. Global Trade Flows, 1982 and 1992

Trade flows	1982	1992	Average annual change
	Billions of dollars		Percent
Total trade in services	405	1,000	9.5
OECD	290	760	
Rest of world	115	240	
Total merchandise trade	1,882	3,731	7.1
OECD	1,174	2,675	
Rest of world	708	1,056	
	Percent		
Share of services in total	17.7	21.1	1.8
OECD	19.8	22.1	
Rest of world	14.0	18.5	

institutional decisions and understandings. The architecture of the GATS therefore differs significantly from that of the GATT (see box 4-1).[4]

Services are defined in the GATS to include any service in any sector except those supplied in the exercise of governmental functions.[5] The Agreement applies to four "modes of supply:" (1) cross-border supply of a service (that is, not requiring the physical movement of supplier or consumer); (2) provision implying movement of the consumer to the location of the supplier; (3) services sold in the territory of a member by (legal) entities that have established a presence there but originate in the territory of another member; and (4) provision of services requiring the temporary movement of natural persons (service suppliers or persons employed by a service supplier who is a national of a country that is a party to the agreement).[6] The concept of a barrier to trade is consequently wider in the GATS than in the GATT (see also box 4-2). In addition to tariffs and quotas, policies restricting FDI and regulatory regimes are of direct interest. The GATS is the first multilateral trade agreement to recognize that nondiscriminatory regulatory regimes may nonetheless act to

---

4. See Hoekman and Sauvé (1994) for a more comprehensive discussion of the GATS. See Bhagwati (1987), Feketekuty (1988), and Messerlin and Sauvant (1990) for discussions of negotiating positions and issues.

5. Services bought by governments (that is, procurement) are also excluded for the time being from the MFN obligation and the negotiated specific commitments. Negotiations on services procurement are to occur within two years of entry into force of the GATS.

6. This is basically the typology developed by Bhagwati (1984) and Sampson and Snape (1985).

Box 4–1. Basic Principles of the GATT and the GATS

Most-favored-nation treatment

GATT: Requires that a contracting party provide any GATT member treatment no less favorable than that accorded to any other supplier of the same product when imposing tariffs or applying regulations related to the entry/exit of goods into/from its territory. *GATS*: Identical to GATT obligation. A major difference is the one-time possibility to exempt specific industries from the MFN obligation when signing the agreement, an option that does not exist under the GATT.

National treatment

GATT: Requires that foreign goods, once they have entered into the territory of a contracting party—having satisfied whatever customs formalities are applicable, including the payment of customs duties and/or other charges—be treated no less favorably in terms of taxes and measures with equivalent effect than domestic firms. *GATS*: Same as GATT, except that the obligation only applies to service sectors and subsectors that a country decides to list in its schedule of commitments (see below). Even then, the obligation only applies to the extent that the country does not list policies that violate national treatment in its schedule.

Market access

GATT: No obligations exist. *GATS*: Six types of measures are in principle prohibited for sectors that are included in a country's schedule, unless the measures are listed. Most of these measures are regulatory policies that apply equally to foreign and domestic firms.

Definition of trade

GATT: Agreement applies only to cross-border trade. *GATS*: Agreement applies to four modes of supply, including investment.

Schedules of commitments

GATT: Each country must provide a list of its tariffs to the GATT. In principle these are "bound," that is, tariffs cannot be raised above the level listed in its schedule of concessions without incurring a penalty. *GATS*: Each country must list the sectors to which it will apply the national treatment and market access obligations, subject to whatever measures it seeks to maintain that will violate these obligations. Scheduling commitments implies that these are bound. Modifications to schedules require compensation to be "paid."

Dispute settlement procedures

GATT and *GATS* share a common dispute settlement mechanism under the WTO. Cross-retaliation is possible, that is, nonimplementation of a panel decision pertaining to one area may lead to retaliation being authorized in another.

Box 4–2. Barriers to Trade in Services

There are two types of barriers to trade in services, natural and man-made. Natural barriers arise because of the nature of services. Their nonstorability often requires producers and consumers to be in the same place at the same time for a transaction to occur. Their intangibility makes it more difficult for consumers to determine the quality of service providers. In conjunction with the need for interaction between producers and consumers, this makes cultural and linguistic differences more important barriers to trade than is the case in trade in goods. Foreign direct investment is often required to overcome natural barriers to trade in services.

Man-made barriers can be divided into two types, depending on whether they involve discrimination against foreign providers. Discriminatory trade barriers are the same as are applied to goods, examples being tariffs, taxes, or quotas. Of these, quotas are by far the most important, as tariffs are difficult to apply to trade in services because of their intangibility. Quotas are often prohibitive, there simply being a prohibition on trade in a particular service. Insurance is an example of a service where trade is often forbidden, while audiovisual services (broadcasting) may be subject to quotas (programming restrictions). Given the technological constraints on trade in services (that is, the importance of natural barriers to trade), policies relating to foreign direct investment are often of greater importance than traditional trade barriers. Governments may impose performance requirements (such as local content restrictions), or prohibit investment in service activities altogether.

In addition to discriminatory measures restricting access to markets, governments may also impose nondiscriminatory measures that prevent both foreign and domestic firms from entering a market. Examples are limitations on the number of firms that are allowed in an industry, or restrictions on the scope of permitted business. Regulatory regimes, including licensing and certification requirements, even if applied nondiscriminatorily, may effectively prevent trade in services. A key feature of the GATS is that it establishes a framework for addressing policies that restrict inward FDI as well as trade and imposes disciplines on nondiscriminatory regulations that effectively limit access to service markets.

---

restrict access to markets. The GATT, in contrast, deals only with policies that discriminate against foreign goods.

Article II on unconditional most favored nation (MFN) status is a core general obligation of the Agreement: each service or service supplier from a member must be treated no less favorably than any other foreign service or service supplier. MFN applies to all trade in services as defined in article I. Because the level of market openness varies among countries, a binding requirement to apply unconditional MFN was resisted by service industry representatives in a number of industrialized countries. They argued that unconditional MFN would allow countries with restrictive policies to maintain their status quo and "free ride" in the markets of more open countries. Financial service industries from G-7 countries and U.S. telecommunications providers successfully lobbied for including the possibility of invoking MFN exemptions as a way to force sectoral reciprocity. The concept of reciprocity that was used was clearly not the "first-difference" notion of equating marginal reductions in barriers that has been used to very good effect in the GATT. This was due in part to the difficulty of identifying, let alone quantifying, market access restrictions. The use of sectoral reciprocity is unfortunate in that it reduces the scope for cross-sectoral tradeoffs. Its economic rationale is also rather weak. The premise is that the granting of MFN by countries with open markets allows firms originating in markets that are less open to free ride. It is not obvious how realistic this fear is, as presumably such foreign firms can be expected to be less competitive than domestic firms that are operating in a more competitive environment. To the extent that the concern is more one of achieving access to the foreign market, it is unclear why discriminating against foreign suppliers in that particular sector (or threatening to do so) is the appropriate policy, as such suppliers are less likely to be competitive on export markets.[7]

Whatever the rationale, an annex allowing for MFN exemptions was included in the GATS. It specifies that MFN exemptions should in principle be time-bound (lasting no longer than ten years) and are subject to periodic review and negotiation in subsequent trade liberalizing rounds. Exemptions can be invoked only once, upon joining the Agreement. Although the annex does allow pressure to be exerted on countries with more restrictive regimes, and this may have some effect in opening markets, invocation of MFN exemptions clearly will reduce the value of the GATS as a whole. This will be the case in particular insofar as domino effects occur, an exemption by one government leading to a retaliatory exemption by others.

In the final days of the Uruguay Round it became clear that a number of participants were ready to invoke the annex on article II exceptions for financial services, basic telecommunications, maritime transport, and/or audiovisual services. Rather than allow a situation to develop where countries would withdraw conditional offers in these areas and exempt them from the MFN obligation, a compromise solution was reached under which negotiations on a number of these sectors could continue without endangering the establishment of the GATS. A second annex on financial services was included,[8] providing

---

7. Of course, it may be that foreign suppliers are subsidized in some fashion. But invocation of an MFN exemption is a very inferior way of dealing with such a situation.

8. There already was an annex on financial services in the draft agreement. This largely took into account some of the sectoral specificities in the context of the GATS general obligations.

for negotiations on financial services to be concluded within six months of the entry into force of the agreement establishing the WTO. If negotiations are not successful—that is, the market access offers made by certain countries are not satisfactory to other, demandeur, countries—members are free to withdraw conditional offers in this area (invoke an MFN exemption). During the six-month period those countries that have listed exemptions conditional upon the level of commitments taken by other members will not apply them. A decision was also made to continue negotiations on basic telecommunications and maritime transport. These were initiated in May 1994, and are to be concluded by end-April and end-June 1996, respectively. Until then, both the MFN requirement and the possibility of invoking an exemption will not enter into force for these services, except to the extent that a member has made a specific commitment for a sector. Much depends therefore on ongoing negotiations.

The general obligations of the GATS, of which MFN is the most important, are complemented by specific commitments on market access and national treatment. Market access is not defined in the GATS. Instead, agreement was reached on a list of six measures that in principle are prohibited. These consist of limitations on: the number of service suppliers allowed, the value of transactions or assets, the total quantity of service output, the number of natural persons that may be employed, the type of legal entity through which a service supplier is permitted to supply a service (for example, branches versus subsidiaries for banking), and participation of foreign capital in terms of a maximum percentage limit of foreign shareholding or the absolute value of foreign investment. National treatment for foreign services and service suppliers is defined as treatment no less favorable than that accorded to like domestic services and service suppliers. Such treatment may or may not be identical to that applying to domestic firms, in recognition of the fact that in some instances identical treatment may actually worsen the conditions of competition for foreign-based firms (for example, a requirement for insurance firms that reserves be held locally). Although the measures that are prohibited under the market access article are mostly nondiscriminatory, in that they affect foreign and domestic firms equally, they also include discriminatory policies (foe example, percentage limits of foreign shareholdings). The latter will also violate national treatment.

Specific commitments apply *only* to listed service sectors and subsectors, and then only to the extent that sector-specific qualifications, conditions, and limitations are not maintained. Any or all of the six types of measures that are prohibited in the market access article may continue to be applied to a sector

Figure 4–1. Format for Country Schedules of Specific Commitments under the GATS

Sector or subsector	Mode of supply	Conditions and limitations on market access	Conditions and qualifications on national treatment	Additional commitments
	Cross-border trade			
	Commercial presence (FDI)			
	Movement of consumer			
	Movement of personnel			

that is listed by a country as long as these measures are also listed. Moreover, these measures can pertain to any or all of the four modes of supply. Figure 4-1 illustrates the rather confusing format of country schedules of specific commitments used in the GATS. The distinction made between general and specific obligations, the scheduling of specific commitments by sector and exceptions to those commitments by mode of supply, and the allowance for MFN exemptions implies that the impact of the GATS very much depends on the content of the country schedules and the extent to which MFN exemptions are invoked. In comparison with the GATT, general rules and principles are less important.

The structure of the GATS implies that negotiations in the services area were (and will be) sectoral, and they will likely be driven by the concerns and interests of the major players in each industry. Although national treatment of foreign suppliers and elimination of nondiscriminatory barriers to market access are required under the GATS, these rules apply on a sector-by-sector, country-by-country basis. This is a major difference from the GATT. The sectoral approach was probably unavoidable, given the widely differing regulatory regimes across countries and sectors. It is important to note in this connection that a generally applicable national treatment rule in an agreement covering both trade and establishment would be equivalent to free trade (abstracting from nondiscriminatorily applied regulations such as those listed in the market access article). Less understandable is why exceptions to national treatment needed to be linked to all four modes of supply.

Several problems can be identified with respect to the design of the scheduling of specific commitments under the GATS. All of these may prove detrimental to the functioning of the agreement and could affect the prospects for future multilateral liberalization by slowing down its pace. The combination of having to list the sectors subject to the market access and national treatment articles, but also allowing a listing of nonconforming measures that will continue to be maintained is not conducive to transparency. The GATS generates no information on sectors, subsectors, and activities in which *no* commitments are scheduled—most often the sensitive ones in which restrictions and discriminatory practices abound. This is a serious shortcoming when one considers the nature and origin of impediments to trade in the services area (that is, regulatory barriers at both the national and the subnational levels).[9] Countries are also granted significant degrees of regulatory discretion in terms of maintaining measures that may depart from otherwise bound undertakings. For example, commitments relating to commercial presence may be subject to the right to maintain or impose authorization and/or screening procedures, and the criteria or specific measures that underpin such procedures may not necessarily be clearly defined or specified in the schedule.

Scheduling commitments according to modes of supply may also create certain incentive effects. Somewhat ironically, given the early resistance to discussing investment-related matters in the Group of Negotiations on Services (GNS), the bulk of commitments lodged under the GATS, especially by developing countries, relate to the commercial presence mode of supply. Indeed, the decision to schedule by modes of supply allows governments to maintain or impose de facto trade-related investment measures (TRIMs). By only scheduling commercial presence as a mode of supply for a particular service sector, foreign service providers can be compelled to establish an in-country presence as a prerequisite for market access, even if cross-border trade is feasible and more efficient.[10] While such TRIMs are, of course, negotiable in future rounds, a more neutral approach to scheduling would have made such distortions less easy to impose.

As mentioned earlier, market access is not defined in the GATS, there being instead a closed list of in principle prohibited measures. The measures that are prohibited will frequently reflect a country's regulatory regime. For example, governments may impose limitations on the number of firms in the context of

---

9. See Hindley (1987), Hoekman (1994), Sapir (1993), and Snape (1993) for discussions of barriers to trade and determinants of market structure in service industries.

10. The introduction of modes of supply as a variable can greatly complicate the political economy of the negotiating process (Hoekman, 1994). In practice, many governments appear to have a preference for FDI, for reasons of employment and value-added creation and regulatory control.

"natural monopolies" or public utilities. What matters then is not the limitation per se, but how contestable markets are. If a government periodically auctions licenses, are the limitations on the number of firms (licenses) a market access barrier? As it is worded the market access article gives a foreign firm the opportunity to use article XVI as the justification for a complaint to the WTO independent of the degree of contestability of a regulated market. This is because the article focuses on the form of measures, not on their effect.[11] The scope for disputes (that is, the need for interpretation by panels) appears great in this connection. The same applies with respect to allegations that national treatment commitments have been violated. Many sectors will continue to be subject to scheduled measures that violate national treatment but that may be worded somewhat ambiguously, again complicating dispute settlement. The history of GATT dispute settlement cases relating to disciplines that were less than clearcut (for example, agricultural export subsidies) suggests that there is the potential for some controversy.

In comparison with the GATT, dispute settlement in the GATS is likely to rely less on fundamental principles or concepts. Instead, interpretation of country schedules can be expected to form an important part of the panel process. This may increase the number of cases as it reduces the scope for one panel finding to have a general impact in terms of interpreting the rules. Insofar as interpretation of schedules does indeed turn out to be a significant burden on the WTO's dispute settlement body, it can be noted that nothing in the GATS compels members to schedule commitments by mode of supply. In principle, therefore, a more transparent approach to scheduling of commitments might be followed in future negotiations, involving the elimination of the distinction. Given that an essentially sectoral approach will be pursued, an alternative approach might focus on negotiating commitments relating to previously identified, specific needs of service providers in a given sector (for example, access to capital, information, telecommunications networks, or accompanying labor mobility). Much will depend in this connection on the experience that is obtained with the GATS in the coming years, on the case law that will be developed through the functioning of the dispute settlement process, and on the functioning of agreements such as the NAFTA, which do not schedule commitments by mode of supply (see below).

---

11. The article prohibits specific measures only. It would have been strengthened, and dispute settlement facilitated, if the words "or measures with equivalent effect" had been added. European Union (EU) experience in enforcing the Treaty of Rome has demonstrated the importance of this.

It is unclear what is the magnitude of liberalization that was achieved on services. In part this is because all the country schedules were not yet publicly available at the time of writing. However, the preliminary offers that were on the table as of mid-1993 covered around one-fifth of developing country service sectors and some two-thirds of industrialized country service markets. Given that some of what was provisionally on the table may be withdrawn (depending on ongoing sectoral negotiations), it is clear that many services will not even in principle be subject to the market access and national treatment commitments. Also, the "effective" coverage of country liberalization will be substantially less than is suggested by simple sectoral coverage, as this must be discounted with whatever restrictions on national treatment and market access continue to be maintained. Moreover, account must be taken of the so-called headnotes found in many schedules that maintain (restrictive) regulations that apply across a number of subsectors or modes of supply. In all cases, national laws and regulations remain applicable, and the economic impact of regulatory regimes will differ across countries in ways that are difficult to determine. Finally, as mentioned earlier, there are ongoing negotiations regarding financial services that will influence the coverage of the GATS in the short run (mid-1995) and the medium term (basic telecoms and maritime transport). All in all, it will often be difficult to determine whether a schedule even goes so far as to imply a standstill (that is, locks in the status quo).

GATS and Regional Integration

The GATS is similar to the GATT in permitting signatories to pursue preferential liberalization arrangements, subject to a number of conditions that are intended to minimize potential adverse effects on nonmembers as well as on the multilateral trading system as a whole. Three conditions are imposed on economic integration agreements involving GATS Members. First, they must have "substantial sectoral coverage." This contrasts with the "substantially all trade" requirement of the GATT, suggesting that the drafters of the GATS intended it to be less restrictive than the GATT. This conclusion can also be drawn with respect to the other two conditions. Thus the second requirement is that integration agreements are to eliminate substantially all discrimination between or among the parties to the agreement in sectors subject to multilateral commitments. More precisely, what is required is the elimination of existing discriminatory measures and/or the prohibition of new or more discriminatory measures. A mere standstill agreement may therefore be sufficient. Third, such agreements are not to raise the overall level of barriers to trade in services originating in other GATS members within the respective sectors or subsectors compared to the level applicable before such an agreement. As no distinction is made between customs unions and free trade areas in the GATS, countries participating in a free trade area (by far the likeliest scenario) may be permitted to raise some barriers against nonmembers, as long as the overall level of barriers of all the members of the agreement vis-à-vis nonmembers, for each of the relevant sectors or subsectors, does not increase. This again contrasts with the GATT, which prohibits such rebalancing for members of a free trade area, unless compensation is offered to affected GATT contracting parties.

The weakness of the disciplines on regional economic integration imply only a limited constraint on "strategic" violations of the MFN obligation and the specific commitments on market access and national treatment made under the GATS. The absence of any requirement that integration agreements be open in principle to the accession of third countries is noteworthy and unfortunate. While this may reflect in part a symmetry constraint—article XXIV of the GATT has no such requirement—augmenting the GATT's rules in this regard would have been equally beneficial.

GATS as an Anchor

In evaluating the GATS, an important consideration is its likely impact on—usefulness to—countries seeking to enhance the economic efficiency of their service industries. Participation in a multilateral agreement imposing certain disciplines and constraints on national policy formation may help a government in pursuing or implementing desired changes in domestic policies. Membership in the GATS may both increase the credibility of reform and help governments resist demands from politically influential interest groups to alter policies in the future. In part this is because the GATS imposes costs on "backsliding." Member states may only withdraw specific commitments after negotiation with—and compensation of—affected parties. In the event such negotiations result in inadequate offers of compensation for affected parties, the GATS foresees arbitration. If the member state withdrawing a specific commitment does not comply with the suggestions of the arbitration panel, retaliation may follow.

But this is all conditional upon significant liberalization having occurred. Will membership in the GATS help governments pursue liberalization efforts? The standard rationale for the pursuit of multilateral (reciprocal) liberalization efforts is that increased access to foreign markets is likely to be of interest to domestic export-oriented industries, and that these are then given an incentive to oppose lobbying by import-competing industries against the opening of domestic markets. This political dynamic is arguably less strong in the GATS context because many of the services in which developing countries are likely to have or develop a comparative advantage require movement of labor (natural persons). This is the mode of supply that has mostly been kept off the table by industrialized countries, few offering significant increases in market access opportunities. It remains unclear what will eventually emerge from the GATS in this connection, as negotiations are still ongoing on issues relating to movement of natural persons supplying services.

The main need for most developing countries is to liberalize access to their service markets, thereby reaping efficiency gains as firms and consumers obtain access to lower priced, higher quality services. The issue is what the GATS does to help a government liberalize in the face of opposition by powerful domestic lobbies. The nongenerality of national treatment is an important negative factor in this connection, as is the sector-specificity of market access commitments. A government cannot tell its lobbies that it must join the GATS, and that this means it must automatically abide by the national treatment principle for all sectors and offer foreign firms access to service markets. Instead, it must explicitly list each and every sector to ensure that national treatment and market access obligations will apply. This clearly makes matters much more difficult for governments that need an external justification for resisting protectionist pressures.

More generally, GATS imposes few limitations on national policy, only requiring that no discrimination across alternative sources of supply occurs. It allows parties to implement policies that are detrimental to—or inconsistent with—economic efficiency. A good example is the article specifying the conditions under which measures to safeguard the balance-of-payments may be taken, such measures rarely being efficient. It can also be noted that the GATS does not require a participating country to alter the regulatory structure of certain service sectors, or to pursue an active antitrust or competition policy. Liberalization of trade and investment may need to be augmented by regulatory change (frequently deregulation) and an effective competition policy in order to increase the efficiency of service sectors such as finance, transportation, and telecommunications. If liberalization is simply equated with increased market access for (certain) foreign suppliers, this may have little effect in markets that are characterized by a lack of competition. The main result will then simply be to redistribute rents across firms.

GATS Compared with NAFTA

In evaluating the GATS (or the TRIPs agreement for that matter), it is helpful to compare it with the NAFTA.[12] It is often held to be a truism that negotiating trade agreements is easier in a small numbers setting and that greater liberalization can be attained among a small group of relatively like-minded countries. There are fairly significant differences between the GATS and the NAFTA. One such difference relates to the extent to which the reach of liberalization instruments and principles is restricted for individual sectors or measures. In the GATS, for example, national treatment, market access, and the right of nonestablishment (that is, the right to provide cross-border services without an established presence) are not general obligations, whereas they are under the NAFTA. Moreover, no distinction is made regarding modes of supply as far as rights and obligations are concerned in the NAFTA. The chapter dealing with trade in services only uses the concept of modes of supply to define such trade. The chapter addressing investment applies to both goods and services.

Another difference pertains to determination of the coverage of the agreements. The NAFTA employs a negative list approach to coverage (that is, all services are covered unless they are explicitly excluded in an annex); the GATS employs positive lists (that is, obligations apply only to listed services). While either approach can lead to the same liberalization outcome, a negative list is significantly more transparent because it forces parties to reveal all nonconforming measures and excluded sectors. Thus, the freedom of GATS members not to list particular service sectors virtually excludes sensitive industries from its coverage without shedding light on the discriminatory practices they maintain in such sectors.

The NAFTA goes beyond the GATS as far as government procurement is concerned. The GATS does not cover government procurement of services, simply calling for negotiations on this issue to be initiated within three years of the entry into force of the agreement.[13] The NAFTA requires covered entities to open public contracts to North America-wide tendering. Disciplines of openness, transparency, and competitive bidding are to apply to the purchases by public entities of goods and services, including construction services. This is significant in that procurement typically represents the most direct and

---

12. For a detailed comparison, see Hoekman and Sauvé (1994).

13. It should be noted that the revised GATT Government Procurement Agreement was expanded to include services. However, this is a plurilateral agreement that binds only signatories (mostly OECD countries).

immediate means of liberalizing the provision of many services—such as computer services, consulting engineering, or construction—that are otherwise subject to few or no cross-border impediments. For such services, the trade-disciplining rules contained in the Agreement's cross-border services chapter may on the whole be less important from the point of view of securing effective access to other countries' markets. The NAFTA takes a positive list approach to entity coverage and a negative list approach for services coverage. Services that are excluded in whole or in part include transportation, storage, communications, finance, R&D, and legal, education and health services.[14]

Neither agreement imposes significant general disciplines on subsidization practices targeted towards service industries. Indeed, the GATS goes further than the NAFTA in this respect by subjecting subsidies to the Agreement's general obligations (that is, transparency, most-favored-nation treatment and dispute settlement). The NAFTA and the GATS are also similar in that neither has services-specific dispute settlement procedures. Potential disputes are subject to a generic set of procedures applying to all matters covered by the NAFTA and the WTO, respectively. The agreements are also similar in that the ultimate sanction is retaliation.

Summing up, while there are certainly similarities between the two agreements, there are also significant differences between the NAFTA and the GATS, especially in the approach taken towards liberalization (negative versus positive listing, scheduling by mode of supply under the GATS, inclusion of procurement under the NAFTA). These differences may in part be a reflection of the fact that the NAFTA addresses both trade and investment in services and goods. The GATS deals only with services. Insofar as it proves possible in the future to extend the reach of the WTO to policies affecting investment along NAFTA lines, an opportunity may be created to rationalize the GATS' approach to scheduling specific commitments.

The TRIPs Agreement

Despite its differences with its older sister, the GATS is clearly modeled on the GATT. That is, an attempt was made to agree to general rules and principles relating to trade policies and to obtain country-specific liberalization

---

14. While the detailed new rules and market opportunities afforded by the NAFTA's procurement chapter are significant, the Agreement liberalizes access to slightly less than one-tenth of North America's estimated $800 billion civilian procurement market.

commitments. No harmonization of policies was pursued. This is in marked contrast with the TRIPs agreement, which establishes minimum standards of intellectual property protection that must be achieved by all members of the WTO. The TRIPs agreement is noteworthy in the multilateral trade context in that it obliges governments to take positive action to protect intellectual property rights. The GATT and the GATS do not require governments to pursue specific policies; they merely impose disciplines on signatories regarding the types of policies they may pursue. The question of whether seeking harmonization of policies and regulatory regimes that indirectly affect trade is a desirable approach in the multilateral context has attracted increasing attention recently.[15] Abstracting from the important normative issues, the TRIPs agreement, as well as the agreement relating to sanitary and phyto-sanitary measures (regulations), illustrates that multilateral agreement on minimum standards is possible.[16] The approach taken is somewhat analogous to a directive in the EU context: the Agreement specifies certain objectives (minimum standards), but leaves it to signatories to determine how these requirements will be implemented.[17]

Protection of intellectual property (IP) was not a completely new issue for trade negotiators. During the Tokyo Round the European Community (EC) and the United States had already tabled a draft agreement on trade in counterfeit goods. Moreover, these two major traders pursued unilateral trade policies to offset perceived instances of inadequate IP protection by trading partners.[18] Indeed, the latter were an important factor inducing developing countries to agree to include IP on the agenda of the Uruguay Round. Negotiators could draw upon over a century of experience with multilateral cooperation in the IP field.[19] An international agency—the World Intellectual Property Organization

---

15. See Bhagwati (1994a).

16. For economic analyses of the desirability of harmonization in the field of IP protection for different types of countries, see Deardorff (1993) and Maskus and Eby-Konan (1994) and the references cited therein.

17. Article 1: "Members shall be free to determine the appropriate method of implementing the provisions of this Agreement within their own legal system and practice."

18. Section 301 and 337 investigations in the United States and the EC's regulation 2641/84 on illicit commercial practices are important examples. Violations or nonenforcement of intellectual property rights have figured prominently in both 301 and regulation 2641/84 actions. In part recourse to unilateral instruments reflected the fact that the International Court of Justice, the main dispute settlement forum in this area, requires a compromise between the interested parties to submit the case to it. See Mavroidis (1993).

19. The Paris Convention for the Protection of Industrial Property dates back to 1883; the Berne Convention for the Protection of Literary and Artistic Works was adopted in 1886.

(WIPO)—providing a forum for the negotiation of substantive obligations with respect to IP already existed. The main problems were that membership of WIPO was not universal and that the organization lacked an adequate enforcement/dispute settlement mechanism for disputes relating to the conventions under its aegis. The TRIPs agreement creates a binding enforcement mechanism for signatories of international conventions on IP.

TRIPs differs from the GATS in that it is a much more solid and transparent agreement.[20] TRIPs includes many more substantive obligations. National treatment and MFN are general obligations with regard to the protection of IP that must be satisfied within one year of the entry into force of the Agreement by all members.[21] Obligations regarding six types of IP are specified, including protection of *trademarks* (to last at least seven years; equal treatment to be given to service and trade marks; prohibition on compulsory licensing), *geographical indications* (prohibition on indications that mislead or constitute "unfair" competition), *industrial designs* (duration of protection of new and original designs to be at least ten years; no protection required for designs dictated essentially by technical or functional considerations), and *layout designs of integrated circuits* (duration of protection at least ten years; protection to extend to products embodying layout design infringements; allowance of compulsory licensing).

In the area of *copyright*, members are required to comply with the substantive provisions of the Berne Convention (1971), with the exception of its obligations regarding the protection of moral rights. The TRIPs agreement goes beyond the Berne convention by providing for rental rights and protection against unauthorized recording of live performances. Computer software is to be protected as a literary work under the Berne Convention. Copyright protection is to last for at least fifty years. Criminal procedures and penalties are to be applicable to copyright abuses (piracy) on a commercial scale. Last but not least, as regards *patent protection,* all signatories are to comply with the substantive provisions of the Paris Convention (1967). Patent protection is to

---

20. Space constraints prohibit a lengthy description of the contents of the agreement. What follows focuses on the most important aspects. See, for example, Cottier (1991), Reinbothe and Howard (1991), Braga (1989), Greenaway and Sapir (1992), and Maskus (1990) for analyses of the issues and negotiating positions.

21. Exceptions to national treatment or MFN are allowed only if an existing international convention on IP specifies a different approach, if rights are involved that are not addressed by the TRIPs agreement, or, in the case of MFN, if there are international agreements that pre-date the entry into force of the WTO.

be provided for almost all inventions and is to be of at least twenty years duration after the date of filing. The twenty-year lower bound implies harmonization toward the standards maintained by industrialized countries.[22] This will have implications for many developing countries that either do not provide patent protection for certain goods or processes, or grant patents of relatively short duration.[23] Patents are required to confer specified exclusive rights to their owners.

Virtually any invention should be patentable. The only exceptions allowed are if commercial exploitation of a patent would be prohibited for reasons of public order or morality, and in order to protect human, animal, or plant life or health or to avoid serious prejudice to the environment. Diagnostic, therapeutic, and surgical methods; plants and animals other than micro-organisms; and essentially biological processes for the production of plants or animals may also be excluded from patentability.[24] The latter exception follows the practice in many European countries, which, in contrast to the United States, do not recognize the patentability of plants and animals. The compromise that was reached on this issue is reflected in the statement that the relevant provision of the TRIPs agreement in this regard is to be reviewed four years after the entry into force of the WTO. Those developing countries that as of the entry into force of the Agreement did not accord patent protection for certain technologies or types of products have ten years to bring their legislation into conformity with the TRIPs requirements.

Compulsory licensing of patents or government use of patents without the authorization of a patent holder remains a possibility, but subject to a number of conditions. These include requirements that right holders be paid "adequate remuneration . . . taking into account the economic value of the [use] authorization" (article 31:h), and that remuneration decisions are subject to judicial or other independent review. The scope for compulsory licensing is not precisely

---

22. In the United States the duration of patents is currently seventeen years from the date the patent is granted. On average, it takes three years to obtain the patent, so that de facto if not de jure the United States meets this condition. Interestingly, NAFTA, in contrast to TRIPs, makes allowance for the U.S. idiosyncracy by specifying either twenty years from filing or seventeen years from the date the patent is granted as being equivalent (Braga, 1993).

23. For example, the patent length for pharmaceutical production processes granted in India was only seven years as of the late 1980s, whereas no patents were provided at all for pharmaceutical products (Reinbothe and Howard, 1991).

24. However, plant varieties must be protectable by patents and/or an effective sui generis system. Thus, countries that do not satisfy this requirement must adapt their legislation. No time period for protection of varieties is specified.

defined. In the absence of a national emergency situation, a necessary condition is that efforts are first made to obtain authorization from the right holder "on reasonable commercial terms." Claims of "excessive pricing" (that is, abuse of dominant position to use the terminology of competition law) may give rise to compulsory licensing. However, article 27:1 appears to eliminate the possibility that lack of local working of a patent can be sufficient grounds for compulsory licensing. That is, importation satisfies patent working requirements.[25] Article 8:1 of TRIPs permits, as a general principle, members to "adopt measures necessary to protect public health and nutrition, and to promote the public interest in sectors of vital importance to their socio-economic and technological development," subject to the condition that such measures are consistent with the provisions of the Agreement.

Article 8:2 goes on to permit members, subject to the same condition, to take "appropriate measures" to prevent the abuse of IP rights by right holders and to prevent practices from being pursued which "unreasonably restrain trade or adversely affect the international transfer of technology." Member countries may specify licensing practices or conditions in their laws that can constitute an "abuse of intellectual property rights having an adverse effect on competition in the relevant market" (article 40:2). Appropriate measures to prevent or control such practices may be taken. Illustrative examples of such practices that are mentioned include exclusive grantback conditions, conditions preventing challenges to validity, and coercive package licensing. The home country authorities of specific right holders are required to consult with host country authorities seeking to secure compliance with its legislation, subject to confidentiality constraints. What constitutes an "abuse of IP rights" or an "adverse effect on competition" is not specified in the Agreement, and the illustrative list of practices provided is quite short. This may be an area where consultations could prove difficult and disputes may arise.[26]

---

25. Article 27:1 states that ". . . patent rights [must be] enjoyable without discrimination as to the place of invention, the field of technology and whether products are imported or locally produced." There is some disagreement as to whether this ensures that local working requirements are inconsistent with the TRIPs agreement. Some developing countries have argued that this remains possible. However, the language of article 27:1 is relatively clear.

26. As is amply illustrated in the literature (for example, Maskus and Eby-Konan, 1994), market structure and conduct are very important in determining the extent of effective market power of an IP right holder and thus pricing decisions, R&D activity, and so forth. Application of competition law will generally require substantial subjective judgment.

Enforcement and dispute settlement procedures are spelled out in some detail, as this was a key area for all parties concerned. Those countries seeking protection of IP needed to have binding and credible enforcement provisions if they were to forsake unilateral retaliatory action. Likely target countries also had a strong interest in constraining the scope for unilateral actions as much as possible. In principle, given that IP is now subject to multilateral disciplines, unilateral policies such as section 301 in the United States can only be invoked with respect to issues that are not covered by the Agreement. Members must ensure that enforcement procedures are available under their national laws that permit effective action against any act of infringement of IP rights. Procedures must be fair, equitable, and not be unnecessarily complicated, costly, or entail unreasonable time limits or unwarranted delays. No obligation exists to put in place a judicial system for the enforcement of intellectual property rights distinct from the enforcement of laws in general. There are provisions on evidence supporting claims of violation of IP rights, injunctions, damages, right of information, indemnification of defendants, and existence of effective provisional measures to prevent an infringement of any IP right from occurring, and procedures to enable right holders suspecting the importation of counterfeit trademark or pirated copyright goods to lodge an application for the suspension of importation.[27] Signatories are to allow criminal procedures and penalties to be applied in cases of willful trademark counterfeiting or copyright piracy on a commercial scale. Penalties in such cases must include imprisonment and/or fines sufficiently large to constitute an effective deterrent.

Dispute settlement procedures are those of the WTO. The provisions of articles XXII and XXIII of the GATT 1994 as elaborated and applied by the Understanding on Rules and Procedures Governing the Settlement of Disputes apply. However, subparagraphs XXIII:1(b) [nonviolation] and XXIII:1(c) of the GATT will not apply to IP disputes for a period of five years from the entry into force of the WTO Agreement.[28] The TRIPs Council is to examine the

---

27. Applicants may be asked to provide a security or equivalent assurance sufficient to protect the defendant and the competent authorities and to prevent abuse.

28. There are three grounds for a contracting party to invoke GATT (now WTO) dispute settlement procedures and claim that benefits accruing to it directly or indirectly under the general agreement are being nullified or impaired or that the attainment of any objective of the general agreement is being impeded. These are: the failure of another contracting party to carry out its obligations under the Agreement (XXIII:1a); the application by another contracting party of any measure, whether or not it conflicts with the provisions of the Agreement (XXIII:1b); or the existence of any other situation (XXIII:1c).

scope and modalities for article XXIII:1(b) and article XXIII:1(c) complaints and submit its recommendations to the Ministerial Conference for approval. The main issues with respect to enforcement are the extent to which countries will avail themselves of the loopholes in the Agreement (for example, regarding the application of competition law to deal with abuse of IP rights, or the justifications offered for compulsory licensing) and whether countries will abide by and implement panel rulings. Much action on this front cannot be expected in the immediate future, given the length of the transition.

Transitional Periods

All members have one year following the date of entry into force of the WTO to implement the provisions of the TRIPs agreement. Developing countries are entitled to a delay of an additional four years for all provisions of the Agreement with the exception of national treatment and MFN. If countries in the process of transition to a market economy are facing special problems in the preparation and implementation of intellectual property laws, they may also request to benefit from the four-year period. Least-developed countries have ten years to conform with the Agreement, and may request extensions of this period. To the extent that a developing country must extend product patent protection to areas of technology that are currently not protectable in its territory (for example, pharmaceuticals or agricultural chemicals), it may delay the application of the provisions on product patents to these areas for an additional period of five years, bringing the total to ten.

The TRIPs agreement does not require retroactive protection of patents that are currently awaiting permission to be sold. The lack of such so-called pipeline protection implies that pharmaceutical/agro-chemical products or processes that have already been patented but are awaiting regulatory approval for marketing (this takes an average of ten years in the United States: the "pipeline") will, once approved, not be protected in those developing countries that do not currently meet TRIPs requirements in these areas until the transition period has passed.[29] This was a major issue for developing countries as it

---

29. However, countries are to provide a means by which applications for patents can be filed; apply to these applications the criteria for patentability as if they were already being applied; and provide protection as from the grant of the patent for the remainder of the patent term, as of the date of filing. Thus, if an application is filed in 1997, the patent will be enforced as of 2005 for another twelve years.

determined to a great extent the magnitude of the possible welfare loss associated with granting IP protection to pharmaceuticals.[30]

While it has been claimed that these transition periods are long (especially by the pharmaceutical industry in the United States), it should be kept in mind that transition periods for the abolition of the MFA and agricultural liberalization by OECD countries are also long. Implementation of the TRIPs agreement will involve adjustment costs for developing countries. While these costs are not incurred gradually (as is the case with incremental implementation of liberalization commitments on, for example, textiles and clothing), the transition period reduces the aggregate cost.[31] Similarly, while there may remain some "holes" in the TRIPs agreement as far as OECD industry is concerned, these are less large than those allowing, for example, the imposition of contingent protection against developing country exports. A case can be made that as far as the "structural adjustment" associated with the Uruguay Round is concerned, developing countries have committed themselves to doing as much, if not more, on the new IP issue than OECD countries with regard to an old issue such as protection of their textiles and clothing industries.[32]

---

30. See Subramanian (1994) and Maskus and Eby-Konan (1994) for analyses of the possible orders of magnitude involved.

31. There are no definitive empirical estimates of the impact of the TRIPs agreement on developing countries. Much depends in this connection on the dynamic effects of the agreement. The static impact is unambiguously negative for those countries that do not provide patent protection, but even here the magnitude is unknown. Market structure and conduct is very important. However, as noted by one economist, "all evidence and arguments . . . point to the conclusion that, to a first-order approximation, TRIPs is a redistributive issue: irrespective of assumptions made with respect to market structure or dynamic response, the impact effect of enhanced IPR protection . . . will be a transfer of wealth from LDC consumers and firms to foreign, mostly industrial-country firms" (Rodrik, 1994, p. 449). See Maskus and Eby-Konan (1994) for a comprehensive discussion of this issue.

32. This is not to imply that those perceiving a loss from protecting IP will gain from greater access to textiles and clothing export markets. At some level, it seems clear that a tradeoff was made between TRIPs and the rest of the agenda, although it is not possible to identify anything very specific. It is beyond the scope of this paper to address the question of what explains the acceptance by developing countries of the TRIPs agreement, which is more far-reaching than what most observers expected to emerge from the round. One factor that appears to have been important is the regime shift that occurred in the 1980s in attitudes toward inward FDI. As a necessary condition for attracting FDI in certain higher-tech sectors is enforcement of IP, this may have helped change negotiating positions. See Mansfield (1994) for some survey and statistical evidence of the positive impact of host country IP protection and U.S. inward direct investment. Other variables were no doubt the threat of unilateral action on the part of the United States (but also the EU) and the inclusion of the language allowing for compulsory licensing, measures to promote the public interest and the possibility of addressing "abuses of IP rights."

It is perhaps useful in this connection to contrast briefly the provisions of the NAFTA relating to IP with those of the TRIPs agreement. Differences in IP protection in Canada and the United States led to IP being left out of the 1989 Free Trade Agreement (FTA) between Canada and the United States.[33] However, by the early 1990s both Canada and Mexico had reformed their IP laws, greatly reducing the disparity between their legislation and that of the United States. It is unclear to what extent this convergence was motivated by the negotiations on the NAFTA. Clearly, it cannot have been much of a factor in the Canadian case, given earlier nonagreement in the FTA. Nonetheless, the substantial harmonization that occurred before the NAFTA negotiations were initiated could only facilitate the inclusion of IP disciplines. It is of some note, however, that the NAFTA and TRIPs agreements are very similar as far as their substantive obligations are concerned. Indeed, the main difference concerns the issue of transitional periods and, related to this, the absence of pipeline protection under TRIPs. The NAFTA provisions on IP entered into effect immediately after its entry into force and granted pipeline protection as of July 1, 1991.[34] But, as noted earlier, the lack of a transitional period is not surprising. There was not much of a reason for it, given the prior convergence of IP regimes. This is certainly not the case in the multilateral context, where many developing countries must make large changes to their legislation and administrative institutions. Given the current differences in IP protection at the multilateral level, the similarity of the two agreements is striking.

U.S. Objectives and Negotiated Outcomes

The initial U.S. proposal to the GNS centered on five elements: transparency of regulations and procedures affecting trade in services, nondiscrimination (that is, MFN), national treatment, market access, and disciplines on state-sanctioned monopoly providers of services. MFN was to apply to all signatories to the agreement, but not to nonmembers. National treatment was considered to be a fundamental element of any agreement and was to be a binding, general obligation. While the existence of national monopolies was accepted, the United States proposed that such entities be required to provide services to foreign firms on a nondiscriminatory basis. Trade was to be defined broadly, including not just cross-border transactions but also FDI (commercial

---

33. See Braga (1993).
34. See Braga (1993).

presence), as this was considered to be crucial to ensure market access. All measures limiting market access for foreign service providers were to be put on the table. At the time (late 1987), many developing countries felt that the U.S. submission went beyond the mandate of the GNS.

Early in the negotiations both the EC and major developing countries expressed a preference for an agreement with "soft" obligations—the EC arguing that national treatment should only apply to specific sectors, major developing countries opposing even that. Throughout 1989 and 1990 developing countries consistently defended the need for preferential access to industrialized country markets and the concept of limited reciprocity (that is, being allowed to liberalize fewer sectors). A February 1990 paper submitted by a number of Latin American states—including Brazil, Chile, and Mexico—is representative. It identified a number of ways through which developing countries might be accorded preferential treatment in line with meeting the objective of economic development. These included the right to pursue policies to foster service exports, a general reservation of the right to grant subsidies to domestic service sectors, making market access concessions conditional on permission for developing countries to exempt export subsidies from a national treatment obligation, tolerating the formation of preferential trading arrangements among developing countries, financial aid for technical assistance relating to matters covered by a services agreement and to foster the development of service sector infrastructure, and obligations on industrialized countries to bind and progressively reduce discrimination in government procurement practices. Much of this was eventually incorporated into the draft final act of the Uruguay Round.

At the end of the day the original EC/developing country preference for a soft framework agreement prevailed. While the nongenerality of national treatment and market access obligations reflects the preferences initially expressed by the EC, the positive list approach to the sectoral coverage of the specific commitments was the result of developing country opposition to a negative list. A negative list approach to coverage was proposed by the United States in late 1989 and was supported by the EC. It appears that one element of the deal that was made in obtaining agreement from developing countries to accept a broad definition of trade in services for purposes of the GATS was the adoption of a positive list approach to coverage of the specific commitments. In part this reflected a fear on the part of developing countries that the latter would have imposed too great an administrative burden. A negative list approach—that is, generally binding obligations for all sectors with the exception only of listed services—requires all sectors for which exemptions will be sought to be scheduled.

Although the approach taken in the GATS toward national treatment is consistent with the original desire of the EC not to have general binding obligations in this respect, this had also become the U.S. position. Moreover, while the United States consistently defended the need to have an MFN obligation, it was largely responsible for the inclusion of the annex allowing members to invoke exceptions to MFN. As the negotiations progressed the U.S. negotiating stance regarding the sectoral coverage of the agreement also changed. Pressures emerged from U.S. service industries that were not willing to see access to their markets liberalized (for example, maritime shipping), and bureaucratic turf tussles also impinged upon the initial objective of negotiating a comprehensive, clean agreement (for example, the opposition by the U.S. Treasury to the inclusion of financial services). Finally, the broad agreement of trade (four modes) and the inclusion of the concept of market access reflected the initial U.S. desire for a far-reaching agreement. Thus, the GATS that emerged at the end of the day is pretty close to what the United States wanted, with the probable exception of the positive list approach to determining the coverage of the market access and national treatment obligations. Mention should also be made of the possibility of sectoral cross-retaliation in the dispute settlement area. Where clearly less was achieved than desired is in the magnitude of liberalization commitments made by U.S. trading partners. It was unrealistic to expect very much in this connection, however, given that in many cases the United States is a *demandeur*. It should be kept in mind that a significant amount of unilateral liberalization of service markets occurred in many parts of the world during the 1980s. Of greater immediate importance than further incremental liberalization by specific countries is the extent to which the GATS manages to lock in these changes. Further opening of service markets of interest to U.S. industries can be sought in future negotiating rounds under GATS auspices.

Turning to TRIPs, it appears that the United States (or rather U.S. pharmaceutical, entertainment, and informatics industries, which after all were responsible for getting TRIPs on the agenda) obtained much, if not most, of what was desired when the negotiations were launched. U.S. industries sought multilaterally agreed minimum standards of IP protection in GATT member countries, an obligation to enforce such standards, and the creation of an effective multilateral dispute settlement process. This wish list was widely seen as being very (if not overly) ambitious by many observers at the time. Initial opposition by developing countries was strong. In the event, the industries obtained most of what was sought. The TRIPs agreement may not be perfect from the perspective of U.S. industry—as reflected in the existence of transition periods, the absence of pipeline patent protection and the fact that patentability of plants/animals is not required.[35] But it is clear that very much was achieved in terms of negotiating an agreement with substantive obligations and few loopholes. It is fair to say that developing countries agreed to much more than even an optimist might have hoped for in 1986.

Concluding Remarks

With the negotiation of the GATS and the agreement on TRIPs, the scope of the multilateral trading system and its dispute settlement procedures has been greatly expanded. The two agreements are very different, largely reflecting the fact that positions on policies affecting service industries were much less clearly defined than those with respect to IP. Only time will tell how effective the GATS will prove in terms of liberalizing world trade in services. Notwithstanding the architectural weaknesses of the GATS, much can be done within its confines if governments prove willing to substantially liberalize international transactions in services. The GATS is just the first step in what it is hoped will prove to be a fruitful path leading to substantial liberalization of international transactions in services. It is the first multilateral trade agreement to cover not just trade per se but also FDI and government policies that do not discriminate against foreign suppliers but do restrict entry into a market. Issues related to market access and policies on FDI have increasingly been generating frictions between large trading nations, most prominently in the context of U.S.-Japan trade relations. The GATS illustrates that market access and establishment questions can be addressed multilaterally. The experience that will be gained from implementing the GATS in the coming years should provide useful lessons on if and how disciplines related to market access might also be incorporated into the GATT.

The TRIPs outcome suggests that multilateral agreement on minimum standards for regulatory policies is possible. Looking to the future, this does not imply that multilateral pursuit of harmonization in other areas that are often mentioned—for example, competition law, environmental policy, labor standards—will be as easily achieved. Leaving aside the very important question of

---

35. Note, however, that the latter is not included in NAFTA either.

the desirability of such harmonization from a global welfare perspective, it is clear that national interests, approaches, and preferences diverge widely on these issues. The frequent references to competition policy criteria, albeit undefined, in the TRIPs agreement and the recognition in the GATS that business practices may restrain competition and thus trade in services (article VIII) implies that competition policy is already on the multilateral agenda. However, in contrast to TRIPs (or the area of sanitary and phytosanitary measures), there is very little in the way of previously negotiated disciplines and institutions that have been dealing with the substantive issues. Consequently, harmonization is not likely to be a very fruitful path, even if it were clear (which it is not) that this would be desirable.[36]

Comment by Jagdish Bhagwati

Bernard Hoekman's excellent paper addresses insightfully two of the "new issues" that were included in the Uruguay Round: intellectual property (IP) protection and trade in services. The former agreement is usually called TRIPs (trade-related intellectual property rights), reminding us that the central argument concerning the inclusion of this issue in the GATT was the notion that IP protection was "trade-related" in some way and hence properly belonged there. The latter agreement is called the GATS (the General Agreement on Trade in Services), apparently parallelling the GATT but also avoiding for obvious reasons the more apt characterization that would lead to the acronym GAS (the General Agreement Services).

Of course, the Uruguay Round included other "trade-related" issues, chiefly TRIMs: the trade-related investment measures, principally the proscription of local content and export requirements. But the reason for taking only the TRIPs and GATS together in Hoekman's paper is clearly that the WTO will technically be the overarching umbrella for three main agreements: GATT on trade in goods, GATS, and TRIPs.

Hoekman's analysis of the TRIPs and GATS agreements is particularly interesting and revealing when he compares and contrasts them (especially the GATS) with the GATT on matters such as MFN exceptions, measures con-

---

36. See Bhagwati (1994a) and Hoekman and Mavroidis (1994) for further discussion.

cerning access to markets, and the sectoral nature of the commitments, and their implications. Rather than qualify Hoekman's analysis with minor quibbles, I would like to supplement it instead with some remarks prompted by reflecting on the paper's theme.

Asymmetries

Regarding asymmetries among the GATT, GATS, and TRIPs, one could add one more of some importance. Trade in services can be regarded as broadly symmetric with trade in goods in that, despite the fact that certain service transactions inherently require international factor mobility in the shape of foreign investment and/or labor mobility (and hence trade in such services is better described as service transactions rather than service trade, and the formal analysis of such transactions must go beyond simple trade between countries with internationally immobile factors), one can broadly assert that noncoercive trade will be a mutual-gain affair—that is, all trading nations will profit from such trade, though of course (as political scientists remind us) the relative gains can be a matter of contention because of "baser" motives such as envy and search for supremacy or power.

However, with IP protection and TRIPs, mutual gain is not the presumption we can work with. Where some countries are consumers and others are producers of the IP, the presumption can well be that of a zero-sum game. In reality, that is likely to be so from the Uruguay Round provisions on IP protection, with the majority of the developing countries losing and many developed countries gaining, according to most impartial observers among the economists.

The reason is that IP protection essentially implies solving for a tradeoff. Putting it somewhat heuristically, once technology exists, it is best to diffuse it costlessly; but doing so when technology must be invented means that you distort the incentive to produce the technology. So, there is an optimum patent period during which IP protection should be provided such that the adverse impact on invention is balanced at the margin with the beneficial impact on diffusion.

Evidently, the patent period will increase with the strength of the "supply-side" effect of not providing IP protection on invention; if it is zero or negligible, then the case for beneficial IP protection weakens greatly, even dies. The econometrics today on this question does suggest that the supply-side effect is negligible. In that case, the IP protection built into the Uruguay Round accords is both suboptimally excessive and in fact amounts to essentially a transfer from the consuming to the producing countries.

And, of course, even when IP protection should be positive, its optimal level will vary among different sectors. This may be not simply because of different supply-side effects but also because of different diffusion effects. Thus, for instance, drugs and medicines may get less IP protection because the advantages of diffusion may be regarded as great because of high social valuation of their benefits for malnourished populations. Thus, uniformity of patent periods is likely then to be more wrong than right, as a working rule of thumb, in contrast to the far stronger case that we economists tend to make for uniformity, rather than nonuniformity, of tariff structures as a policy rule.

None of this is news to readers of the recent analyses of IP protection by some of the best international trade theorists today, chiefly Alan Deardorff, Elhanan Helpman, Gene Grossman, and Dani Rodrik. The Uruguay Round accord on IP protection then cannot be seen in the same light as the GATT and GATS.

I suspect that our negotiators are well aware of this fact. Because it is hard to justify on the Benthamite utilitarian logic that we normally employ to arrive at economic policy recommendations, our negotiators have taken instead to talking about "piracy" and "theft," thus implicitly shifting the logic to one of rights (that is, I invented it so it is mine and I do not have to part from it ever, except on my terms for the good of mankind). Of course, if we were to do that, the case for IP protection does not stop at twenty years; it wold be infinite-lived. The very fact that we put down twenty years means that we are implicitly using a utilitarian criterion while justifying IP protection by a rights criterion. But such is the business of public policy: intellectual coherence is not a necessary ingredient of successful public policy. In defense of our negotiators, and the eventual inclusion of the IP protection on current terms at the GATT/WTO, I would simply say the following:

—given the strength of the lobbying for IP protection, as reflected also in our special 301 provisions, and given the necessity of businessmen's support for the passage of the Uruguay Round in Congress, it is hard to imagine what any other U.S. negotiators would have been able to do;

—the developing countries also realized that, given this strength of feeling and lobbying, they probably would continue to face 301 pressures that the administration could not contain; getting the IP protection into the GATT was the lesser evil;

—the developing countries also realized that multinationals increasingly regarded IP protection as a litmus test of their intention to attract foreign investment; granting it then became a way to provide that assurance and to compete successfully for foreign investment in a world economy where that competition has become a fact of life;

—a major developing country like India also came to realize that it was both a producer (software and movies) and a consumer (drugs and pharmaceuticals) of IP and that its own interest lay in reversing its earlier opposition to IP protection; and

—even if IP protection was going to cost them something, most developing countries saw it in the end as a price they had to pay for the success of the Uruguay Round and hence of the GATT and of multilateralism which is evidently the best defense of the weak against the strong nations.

The Question of Investment Rules

What I just said about the developing countries accepting suboptimally excessive IP protection in order to attract foreign investment should remind us immediately of the well-known fear of a "race to the bottom" which environmentalists and labor unions have been drawing our attention to, when seeking cross-country harmonization of environmental and labor standards. The idea underlying the race to the bottom, of course, is that a Nash equilibrium may be characterized by all countries winding up with lower environmental and labor standards than they would choose in a more efficient cooperative equilibrium.

Somehow, this notion has never been raised recently in regard to the terms and conditions being offered by developing countries to foreign investors. Interestingly, not merely in regard to IP protection, but also in regard to TRIMs, the provisions negotiated have always been those that improve the bargaining ability of the multinationals. If a Martian economist interested in designing an optimal set of rules at the WTO on investment were to be engaged as a consultant, would she not express consternation at such a situation? And would she not insist also that, if restrictions imposed on multinationals are to be removed as impediments to world efficiency in resource allocation, then so should be the numerous subsidies and subventions to attract them? The one-way bias in the rules that we are enacting under TRIPs and under TRIMs is a result of lobbying by the multinationals and the inherent weakness of the developing countries today as they compete for scarce funds.

I would add that regionalism, or rather the FTA approach now fashionable in Washington, accentuates that weakness politically by dividing the developing countries into insiders (Mexico), outsiders who are encouraged as being potentially insiders (Chile, maybe South Korea), and other outsiders.[37]

Services, Mode of Delivery, and MFN

Finally, Hoekman's perceptive discussion of the GATS suggests two further comments.

He shrewdly notes that the modes of delivery chosen in the actual concessions offered opt for the "right to establish" rather than for the (human) providers to go to where the users are. This, of course, fits into the notion that developing countries are agreeable to this asymmetry because they would indeed like foreign investment. But I believe that they would be shortsighted not to press for the labor mobility of the providers as well; I suspect that they would have comparative advantage in several services where small-scale human providers rather than large-scale multinationals are the mode of delivery in the continuum of services within a "sector."

As for the conditional MFN (an oxymoron) issue, I can understand the concerns of the countries which feel that they are open and others are shut and the worry about the free rider problem. The free rider problem is grossly exaggerated, as Michael Finger has reminded us: tariff concessions are usually so narrowly defined as to exclude benefits for those who make few concessions of their own. Perhaps this cannot be done as effectively in the services; but, if so, I have not seen an effective argument to convince me.

As for lack of reciprocal openness in a sector, whether services or goods, which drives the demands for conditional MFN, this is partly a question of "fairness": businessmen just feel that this amounts to unfair competition and it is hard to convince them otherwise; fairness, like beauty, is in the eyes of the beholder.

But the demand is also fed by the economic notion that, if my market is open and yours is closed, then you have two markets and I have one, and that if we are both "symmetric" (that is, identical) firms, you will go down the identical cost curve further, lowering your average cost, and gain advantage over me.

---

37. I have recently developed a theory of the Selfish Hegemon, as against the Altruistic Hegemon of Kindleberger, where the hegemon uses tactics such as FTAs (an incentive strategy) and 301 actions (a punishment strategy) to divide the (smaller) developing nations and secure better bargains at the multilateral bargaining table than the hegemon would obtain if it bargained exclusively in the multilateral format. See Bhagwati (1994b).

CARNEGIE LIBRARY
LIVINGSTONE COLLEGE
SALISBURY, NC 28144

This is the idea that gained ground in the 1980s, and I call it the "1980s Silicon Valley Model." As Douglas Irwin and Peter Klenow have shown recently,[38] for the semiconductor industry, learning by doing is practically automatic and identical across countries: it is as if you were teaching Economics 101 and everyone in the class progressed at an identical rate. This type of "robotic" learning-by-doing is surely not applicable to other industries, but it does provide a good empirical foundation for the 1980s Silicon Valley Model, especially in the import-protection-as-export promotion model of Paul Krugman (which in fact came directly from the complaints of the Silicon Valley Businessmen).

Of course, as I have argued in my 1988 book on *Protectionism*,[39] models are as good as the assumptions you make, and this assumption of symmetric firms that learn at the same rate, simply as a function of output, is an absurd one outside of the narrow class of some Silicon Valley industries. In particular, regulated and protected markets are a particularly bad environment, in general, for learning by doing. We know now, not from ideology, but from empirical arguments and evidence, provided by McKinsey & Co. under the guidance of Martin Baily and Robert Solow, and by Michael Porter at the Harvard Business School, that open markets and deregulation lead to our industries becoming "lean and mean," that by being ahead on the curve of deregulation and openness, we get ahead of others on the curve of competitiveness. As someone put it, you improve your game by playing with others better than yourself, not by choosing sparring partners who are your own class.

So, unlike in the 1980s Silicon Valley Model, embraced then by Krugman, with its resulting emphasis on reciprocity of openness and the need for conditional MFN, the smarter policy in modern Schumpeterian industries is to seek reciprocity simply on "fairness" grounds as a political necessity but not to be obsessed by it, and to push ahead with one's own deregulation and openness unilaterally and without conditional MFN. Our competitors will be able to impede us in their markets, but will lose to us in the vast markets opening up for these industries in the so-called "newly emerging markets," of India, China, Brazil, Mexico, Indonesia, and elsewhere. Our competitors will follow suit with their own deregulation and market opening simply to compete and survive. The greater wisdom and policy sense lies in this spirit of unilateralism; the 1980s Silicon Valley Model must be abandoned as yet another of the follies

---

38. Irwin and Klenow (forthcoming).
39. Bhagwati (1988, pp. 95–96).

perpetrated in the 1980s, even more damaging than the witting and unwitting strengthening of the protectionist hand by the scientifically innovative theory of trade in imperfect product markets. Would that Richard Cobden and John Bright, the great leaders of the League to Abolish the Corn Laws in the mid-19th century and therewith to usher in free trade in Great Britain, who passionately believed that unilateralism was best because others would emulate Britain as her free trade policies brought prosperity,[40] were alive today to bury the decade of the 1980s and to lead us into the rest of the 1990s!

Discussion

There was a very active discussion about the Uruguay Round Agreement on intellectual property (IP). In particular, participants held very different perspectives about the way to view IP related issues. Julius Katz strongly disagreed with Jagdish Bhagwati's characterization of the new IP protection as redistributing benefits from developing to industrial countries. He argued that the real issue was one of property rights, which are being violated through counterfeiting and theft. Thus, he saw a fundamental difference between a ten-year transition period for the abolition of the MFA or the liberalization of agriculture and a transition period in IP protection, which in his view gives countries the right to steal for ten more years (twenty years in the case of developing countries). He believed that international recognition of a right to intellectual property had already existed. IP protection had been attained in exchange for the increased market access which many developing nations sought.

John Jackson disagreed that there is any inherent right to intellectual property. However, he noted that there is a tension in the U.S. Constitution and in the law between the property rights view, and the "functionalist" view that IP protection grants a temporary monopoly so as to pay for innovative activity. The latter view raises the issue of how much protection is needed to ensure an adequate rate of return to stimulate innovation, an issue on which there was

---

40. See Bhagwati (1988), where the different arguments for unilateralism in the nineteenth-century debates are discussed at greater length, Douglas Irwin's joint work with me on this historical research must be acknowledged.

much discussion. Barry Bosworth wondered if protection in U.S. markets wasn't enough to pay for innovation. Paul Wonnacott believed that protection should distinguish between production for domestic sales and production for export. He also pointed out that protection for fifty years or more is not a problem for copyrights—if Shakespeare had never written Hamlet, it would not have been written—but that such long protection is a huge problem for patents—if the Wright Brothers had not flown an airplane, one probably would have flown within six months. David Richardson noted that both the length of a patent and its narrowness or breadth were relevant.

Richardson pointed out that Bhagwati's assertion that additional IP protection under the GATT is not efficiency enhancing, but redistributes benefits away from developing countries, relies on the assumption that innovative activity is insensitive to extending patent protection. He challenged this view, arguing that existing research is "still up in the air." Bhagwati explained that his priors for a low supply response stem from evidence that many other types of supply responses are low, and from his view that oligopolistic firms, in an intensely competitive market, will innovate because their competitors are innovating.

Ferrantino also believed that global enforcement of industrial patents would not be welfare enhancing because the marginal increase in research and developments would not outweigh the loss to consumers from removal of imitations. However, in practice, he expected any redistributive effects to be small. Developing countries can grant narrow patents and create lengthy administrative procedures so that the actual effect of the new patent protection could be very weak. Many other participants agreed that enforcement of the new rules will be difficult.

Jackson raised the question of why developing countries agreed to the new IP rules. He discounted the view that they signed on in exchange for market access concessions, arguing that if they were really opposed to IP protection, such a bargain would not have been worthwhile. He reiterated Bhagwati's point that, by the end of the negotiations, many of them had come around to the view that IP protection was in their own interests. Some saw that their own innovators would benefit from the protection. Others saw IP protection as necessary to attract foreign investment, or to limit unilateral action from the United States.

Claude Barfield focused on Bhagwati's concern that the IP agreement may provide a precedent for future agreements on labor and environmental standards. He agreed that any such agreements were likely to be similar in focusing on enforcement of rules at home and abroad as a basis for trade restrictions. However, he saw an important difference in that, unlike for IP, labor and environmental debates centered around whether to force harmonization of standards, or to support mutual recognition of different systems.

There was also some discussion about the agreement on services. Barfield stated that initially, the United States had not even expected to get services on the table. However, as negotiations proceeded, goals had increased dramatically. Although the United States had ended up with less than hoped for in the middle of the process, significantly more had been achieved than expected at the outset. Katz agreed. However, noting that he joined the negotiations in the middle, he expressed disappointment that there was "no beef" in terms of market access commitments and that the end result had little liberalization but more in the way of structure.

Deardorff noted that for some services, part of the production occurs at the place of sale so that domestic producers would be more likely to compete in home markets with foreign producers who produced abroad. He argued that this may make it politically more difficult to maintain unconditional MFN for trade in services than for trade in goods. However, he believed that on economic grounds, an equally strong case for unconditional MFN could be made for trade in services as for trade in goods.

Finally, Jackson stressed the differences among the many service sectors (tourism, medicine, banking, lawyers services) and argued that early attempts to negotiate a blanket set of rules that could be applied across the board had been inappropriate. He agreed with Hoekman that the move to a sectoral approach was more realistic, but that the existing agreement was simply a first step.

References

Anderson, Kym, and Richard Blackhurst, eds. 1993. *Regional Integration and the Global Trading System*. London: Harvester-Wheatsheaf.

Bhagwati, Jagdish N. 1984. "Splintering and Disembodiment of Services and Developing Nations." *The World Economy* 7: 133–44.

———. 1987. "Trade in Services and the Multilateral Trade Negotiations." *The World Bank Economic Review* 1: 549–69.

See Bhagwati, Jagdish. 1988. *Protectionism*. MIT Press.

———. 1994a. "Fair Trade, Reciprocity and Harmonization: The New Challenge to the Theory and Policy of Free Trade." In *Analytical and Negotiating Issues in the Global Trading System*, edited by Alan Deardorff and Robert Stern. University of Michigan Press.

Bhagwati, Jagdish. 1994b. "Threats to the World Trading System: Income Distirbution and the Selfish Hegemon." Working Paper 695, Columbia University; an earlier version appears in the *Journal of International Affairs*, Spring 1994.

Braga, Carlos Primo. 1989. "The Economics of Intellectual Property Rights and the GATT: A View from the South." *Vanderbilt Journal of Transnational Law*, 22.

———. 1993. "Intellectual Property Rights in NAFTA: Implications for International Trade." In *Beyond NAFTA*, edited by A. Riggs and Tom Velk. Vancouver: Fraser Institute.

Cottier, Thomas. 1991. "The Prospects for Intellectual Property in GATT" *Common Market Law Review* 28: 383–414.

Deardorff, Alan. 1993. "Should Patent Protection Be Extended to All Developing Countries?" In *The Multilateral Trading System: Analysis and Options for Change*, edited by Robert Stern. University of Michigan Press.

Feketekuty, Geza. 1988. *International Trade in Services: An Overview and Blueprint for Negotiations*. Cambridge, Mass: Ballinger Publications.

GATT Secretariat. 1994. "Final Act Embodying the Results of the Uruguay Round of Multilateral Negotiations."Geneva: GATT.

Greenaway, David, and André Sapir. 1992. "New Issues in the Uruguay Round: Services, TRIMs and TRIPs." *European Economic Review* 36: 509–18.

Hindley, Brian. 1987. "Trade in Services Within the European Community." In *Free Trade in the World Economy* edited by Herbert Giersch. Tübingen: J. C. B. Mohr.

Hoekman, Bernard, 1994. "Conceptual and Political Economy Issues in Liberalizing International Transactions in Services." In *Analytical and Negotiating Issues in the Global Trading System*, edited by Alan Deardorff and Robert Stern. University of Michigan Press.

Hoekman, Bernard, and Petros C. Mavroidis. 1994. "Competition, Competition Policy and the GATT." *The World Economy* 17: 121–50.

Hoekman, Bernard, and Pierre Sauvé. 1994. *Liberalizing Trade in Services*. Discussion Paper No. 243. Washington, D.C.: The World Bank.

Irwin, Douglas, and Peter Klenow. Forthcoming. "Learning-by-doing Spillovers in the Semiconductor Industry." *Journal of Political Economy*.

Mansfield, Edwin. 1994. "Intellectual Property Protection, Foreign Direct Investment, and Technology Transfer." IFC Discussion Paper No. 19. Washington, D.C.: The World Bank.

Maskus, Keith. 1990. "Intellectual Property." In *Completing the Uruguay Round,*edited by J. Schott. Washington, D.C.: Institute for International Economics.

Maskus, Keith, and Denise Eby-Konan. 1994. "Trade-Related Intellectual Property Rights: Issues and Exploratory Results." In *Analytical and Negotiating Issues in the Global Trading System*, edited by Alan Deardorff and Robert Stern. University of Michigan Press.

Messerlin, Patrick, and Karl Sauvant, eds. 1990. *The Uruguay Round: Services in the World Economy*. Washington, D.C.: The World Bank.

Reinbothe, Jörg, and Anthony Howard. 1991. "The State of Play in the Negotiations on TRIPs." *European Intellectual Property Review*, 5: 157–64.

Rodrik, Dani. 1994. "Comments on Maskus and Eby-Konan." In *Analytical and Negotiating Issues in the Global Trading System*, edited by Alan Deardorff and Robert Stern. University of Michigan Press.

Sampson, Gary, and Richard Snape. 1985. "Identifying the Issues in Trade in Services." The World Economy 8: 171–81.

Sapir, André. 1993. "The Structure of Services in Europe: A Conceptual Framework." *European Economy*, 3: 83–99.

Snape, Richard. 1993. "Effects of GATT Rules on Trade in Professional Services." In *Coalition and Competition: The Globalization of Professional Business Services*, edited by Yair Aharoni.. London: Routledge.

Subramanian, Arvind. 1994. "Putting Some Numbers on the TRIPs Pharmaceutical Debate." *International Journal of Technology Management* 10: 1–17.

UNCTAD and World Bank. 1994. *Liberalizing International Transactions in Services: A Handbook*. Geneva: United Nations.

Participants

Lewis Alexander
Department of Commerce

Claude Barfield
American Enterprise Institute

Dale Belman
Economic Policy Institute

Nancy Benjamin
International Trade Commission

Jagdish Bhagwati
Columbia University

Barry Bosworth
The Brookings Institution

Ralph Bryant
The Brookings Institution

Susan M. Collins
The Brookings Institution
and *Georgetown University*

Sydney Collins
University of Miami

Lester Davis
Department of Commerce

Alan V. Deardorff
University of Michigan

I. M. Destler
University of Maryland

Robert Devlin
Inter-American Development Bank

William Dickens
The Brookings Institution
and *University of California, Berkeley*

Antoni Estevadeorda
Inter-American Development Bank

Michael Ferrantino
U.S. International Trade Commission

Michael Finger
The World Bank

Isaiah Frank
Johns Hopkins University

Jeffrey Frankel
Institute for International Economics

Bill Frenzel
The Brookings Institution

Joel Goldberg
Department of the Treasury

Joseph A. Greenwald
Consultants International Group

Dale Hathaway
*National Center for Food &
Agricultural Policy*

Noel Hemmendinger
Willkie, Farr & Gallagher

123

1 2 6 4 8

Bernard Hoekman
The World Bank

Lucy Huffman
Department of the Treasury

John H. Jackson
University of Michigan

Timothy E. Josling
Stanford University

Julius L. Katz
Hills & Company
(Former Deputy Director
*Office of the United States Trade
Representative*)

Robert Lawrence
Harvard University

Thea Lee
Economic Policy Institute

Nora Lustig
The Brookings Institution

Warwick McKibbin
Australian National University
and *The Brookings Institution*

Catherine Mann
*Board of Governors of the
Federal Reserve System*

Will Martin
The World Bank

Theodore H. Moran
Department of State

Pietro Nivola
The Brookings Institution

Seamus O'Cleireacain
The Ford Foundation

Peter Orzag
Council of Economic Advisers

Clyde Prestowitz
Economics Strategy Institute

Alfred Reifman
*Congressional Research Service
Library of Congress*

J. David Richardson
Syracuse University and
Institute for International Economics

Martin Richardson
Georgetown University

Steven Schoeny
University of Maryland

Robert Solomon
The Brookings Institution

David Walters
*Office of the United States Trade
Representative*

Peter Wilcoxen
The Brookings Institution
and *University of Texas at Austin*

Paul Wonnacott
Institute for International Economics